HALLMARKS OF A HERITAGE

This book tells of Southern cultures that are very unique to the American design. Many of those customs and beliefs that were established centuries ago still exist today. The reader will journey back into the time when honor and morality was such a respected part of everyday living, when happiness was nurtured by simple things and a good family life was blessed with warm, compassionate and hardworking people.

HALLMARKS OF A HERITAGE will take the reader on mental trips into a picturesque land where nature presides in glorious prehistoric fashion, just as it did thousands of years ago; where the beautiful wild lives in perfect harmony with modern man.... where many forms of enchanting atmospheres are embraced.

There are fascinating legends, prominent mythical characters and exciting festive events that had their beginnings hundreds of years ago and still thrives in grand fashion. And to add a little savorous zest, appetites are teased by those delicious traditional cuisines found no other place on earth.

The book's numerous pencil drawings, writing and poems by Jess DeHart portray factual accounts of lifestyle and behaviors of very distinctive societies. It tells of their trials, hardships, labors and great successes that led to priceless contributions for present generations.

Here, a special segment of American history is related in a manner that is unusually interesting and entertaining.... as it has never before been expressed. There is humor, adventure, tragedy, folklore, religious convictions and legendary cultism.

This book encourages a person's mind to wander into peaceful atmospheres that are pleasantly nostolgic, inspirational and creates images that are embellished with old time flavors.... flavors which are as Southern as Shrimp Creole and Crawfish Pie. It gives new meaning to the word "old-fashioned" and generates special feelings toward a way of life that began many many generations ago and lives on in today's modern world.

HALLMARKS OF A HERITAGE will entertain the mind and stimulate anxieties toward legacies of a unique society that is unparalleled in America... Southern cultures which are cherished with intense passions by those people who are very proud to occupy a privileged place in the America they love so much.

HALLMARKS of a HERITAGE

BY JESS DEHART

New Orleans, Louisiana

HALLMARKS OF A HERITAGE

Library of Congress
Catalog Card Number 83-83113
First Edition April 1984
ISBN 0-913861-00-6

Manufactured in the United States of America
Published and Distributed by Hamlet House
P.O. Box 791044, New Orleans, Louisiana 70179-1044

CONTENTS

CONTENTS *Continued*

ILLUSTRATIONS

ILLUSTRATIONS *Continued*

TREASURED HEIRDOMS

Like fine wines that have mellowed well over the years, many preserved relics of our historical past continue to delight our aesthetic tastes. To attempt to erase from our minds those treasures of our ancestor's age is to try to abandon all duty to preserve our sacred heritage. Having distilled wisdoms of that heritage is to better let us know who we are, where we came from and as a person what we should truly represent in today's society. To be mindful of our past history while looking into the future gives to us a more stable position as an individual, helping us to avoid that status of being just another face in a sea of humanity.... without identity.

Perhaps the happiest and most mentally secure people of our time are those who can relate truly and intimately with a particular sect within a society and still become an important part of the whole; a sect where individual customs, habits and general backgrounds reasonably parallel other certain individuals. Being fully aware of our heritage greatly enhances opportunities to seek out those unique parallels that makes us special.

To appreciate the past and to enjoy historic reminders of years gone by certainly does not mean that we must live in a fantasy of that past. On the contrary, to recognize mistakes made by our ancestors can better prepare us to avoid many blunders and setbacks in our own life. But, at the same time we must not fail to recognize the numerous contributions of our predecessors which could be used favorably to serve our own generations. Many of those so-called antiquated ideas and practices may not be near as primitive and obsolete as most of us may think them to be. Many of them could serve very well to better our lives today. Recognitions in the use and preservation of energy, or the construction of dwellings to better suit local climatic conditions are just two examples of proven practices of the past that are presently becoming very popular in the planning of an efficient and economical tomorrow.

We must not forget that the foundations for this great country were firmly established by our forefathers many generations ago. Without their trials or accomplishments and without their wisdoms America never would have become as great and as independent as she now is. We must not forget the many hardships, sorrows and misfortunes they endured in order to achieve that great goal of freedom; an independence many of them were unable to enjoy. While in the making of this freedom many died for that great privilege we all enjoy; a privilege that most of us seem to take too much for granted. Having become too passive about our beginnings too many think of this sovereignty as having always been here and can never be taken away from us. We must never allow ourselves to become that unmindful of the numerous physical, moral and spiritual gifts handed down by the fathers of this wonderful land.

There are so many remnants left today of the pioneering and developing era of Louisiana. For the most part these reminders are pleasant ones.... some are melancholy in nature. Frequently they relate to us a position played during the infancy and growing up period of this country. Many old homes constitute symbols of the character of the people who built them, many are hallmarks of individual successes and most of them become more beautiful with age.

If we travel the old roadways and bayous through country land, forest, swamp and prairies it is so much easier for us to form clearer pictures within our imaginations and we are better able to understand reasoning and purpose for doing things in ways that they were done during those early years. And, for a time we can reward our minds and our hearts by ridding ourselves of many of the strains of this stressful age by traveling into the tranquil surroundings of the past and reflecting on the many blessings that had helped so much to mold generations of a civilized, compassionate and productive people. This peaceful silence is so very filled with clean refreshing old time atmospheres which are greatly enhanced by the fresh fragrances of nature.... nature in its purest form.

Still remaining are numerous rural mansions, countless Creole and Acadian homes, country stores, sugarhouses, slave cabins, elegant town dwellings and sturdy community structures that have become appropriate monuments to the developers of historic Louisiana. There are many natural parks with peaceful shades of by-gone days that are canopied by gigantic oaks and stately magnolias establishing living testimonials to those settlers who lived nearby. There are memorials to early Louisiana institutions of higher learning and there are numerous churches many many decades old that remain beautiful tributes to yesteryears devoutly religious people of Louisiana. Fabulous Creole and Acadian cuisines attest to the unmatched culinary abilities of colonial Louisiana's "Cuisinieres" who so skillfully created the famous delicious dishes that we now savor with great delight.

It isn't intended that this be a history book on Louisiana, neither does it represent all facets of Louisiana's heritage; that would surely require many more pages than what now exists between these covers. Instead, with this book, the author wishes to entertain the minds and stimulate interests in the legacies of Louisiana. The author has illustrated a number of the more prominent customs, unique behaviors, some of the characters and some of the human realities that existed during the development of Louisiana.

There are cherished reminders of the unhurried peace, joys and entertainments of those early years. And, there are sad memories, superstitions, unsavory behaviors, myths and factual accounts of popular legendary figures. So broad is the scope of Louisiana heritages that within this restricted space the author can only begin to hint some highlights of the cultures, unique postures and distinctive practices that make Louisianians stand out as rare and interesting individuals of America.... proud not to be just another number among multitudes of lonely followers.

Today, the product of the early Louisiana settlers is a product of a novel and separate culture unparalleled in the United States and so uncharacteristic of American design. The natives of Louisiana are very warm, compassionate and fun-loving people with very high values and who are unsurpassed in merits of pride for their unique heritage.

PEOPLE OF EARLY LOUISIANA

J DeHart

A GRAND AND NOBLE LADY

God has given this land to mankind and has delivered to her a people who with a sacred reverence has preserved her riches for many centuries past. Her countless blessings were first awarded to the native indians who so nobly handed down this great wealth to others who had traveled from distant lands to admire, to belong, to love and to defend her; through her veins flow lifebloods of many nations.

Stripped of all masquerades and clothed in her virtues alone she remains unashamed of the qualities that God has granted to her, and with solemn dignity she reveals the many beautiful attributes of her structure. She is the proud queen of lazy bayous, torrential rivers, enchanting swamps, mysterious marsh lands and fertile soils that yield vast quantities of animal and plant life. Her fruitful humus has poured forth an abundance of nourishment into distant lands.

She is the gracious keeper of an Eden of fishes, birds, animals and lush vegetations that has long beckoned a delightful welcome to all of mankind. For many centuries she has fed, clothed and sheltered the multitudes. With feverish passions, early planters came forth to stimulate her soils into producing wholesome foods for the tables of many nations; she has always bore good fruit for all who were privileged to be embraced by her womb.

With an everlasting graciousness she was destined from her very creation to become a tranquil refuge for the restless and the oppressed who seek out a peace with new beginnings and generous rewards in return for their unselfish endeavors. She has offered unto them the strength, ambition and unlimited opportunities for success and happiness with a heritage that is unlike any other.

Bodies of wicked minds from afar have attempted to rape her virtues only to be thrust down by the loyal forces who defend the decency of her morality; there can be no "evil seeds" that can develop into a power capable of destroying her. And, with sovereign dignity she has become the envy of all who have vowed jealously to bring dishonor upon her; with grace, poise and vigor she has repelled all forces of aggression.

This benevolent queen proudly proclaims her bountiful assets, remaining ever so thankful for the immense wealth that God has bestowed upon her and she has unselfishly shared those blessings with a grateful mankind. Her unmeasurable accomplishments will remain immortal, written in with a spiritual pen and never to be erased from the pages of history; she will always be listed as that grand and ever-loving lady with the noble title of "LOUISIANA."

J DeHart

Early Louisiana Indians

The Attakapa, Opelousa, Alabaman, Chitimacha, Chawasha, Houmas, Acolapissa and Washa were indian tribes already in southern Louisiana when the French and Spanish arrived. Choctaw and Koasati tribes arrived in Louisiana after the white man settled north of Lake Ponchartrain and in wooded lands west of New Orleans. Chitimacha, Chawasha and Houmas indians built settlements west and south of New Orleans in the wooded swamplands and along bayous of higher land sections. The Tunica tribes villaged chiefly in an area where the Red River joined the Mississippi, near Marksville and in northeast Louisiana. Caddoans were centered along the upper Red River.

The Opelousa and Alabaman inhabited areas now known as the parishes of St. Landry, Evangeline and Pointe Coupee. Quinipissa and Colapissa tribes were located in the district now known as uptown New Orleans; like the Opelousa, they were friendly and allied with the French during the Indian Wars.

Attakapa tribes camped regularly along Bayou Teche and the Vermilion, Calcasieu and Mermentau rivers, but were of nomadic nature, roaming southern Louisiana in gypsy-like fashion hunting bear and other furbearing animals for trade purposes. The Attakapa were said to be cannibalistic but the more refined and civilized Opelousa and Alabaman united to successfully exterminate the Attakapa tribes. The Natchez Indians, located in various areas east of the Louisiana Territory, were of a hostile nature and in constant conflict with the French and Spanish. Because of those wars, they became extinct in the early years of the white man in Louisiana. They did not have the sophisticated weapons and materials of the white man; this along with few numbers eventually brought annihilation.

To give specific boundaries of locations for any of the various southern Indian Nations would be misleading, due to the erratic habits of most tribes. Many of the southern indians were of a roaming nature and entire villages were said to relocate practically overnight. This was due perhaps to their constant demand for sanitary surroundings as well as the need for new hunting grounds. When wildlife became sparse they moved elsewhere just as they did when searching for more fertile soils for farming.

Most indians of southern Louisiana were clean people, bathing often and diseases resulting from uncleanliness were unkown to them until the white man invaded their world. All hair, with the exception of that which was on the head was permanently removed from the entire body by means of hot shell ashes and hot water treatments. So skilled were they with the method that no scars or ill effects resulted.

During mild weather and summer months men and women alike wore no clothes above the waist; men wore only a breech cloth and the women wore short skirts of grass, fur or skins. Girls to eight years of age and boys to twelve were nude. When winter months demanded, adults as well as children wore skins or fur mantles for protection against the cold. Women of some tribes tatooed flower designs on their shoulders and breasts to make themselves more attractive to their men. Men let their hair grow long and straight and wore headbands while the women usually braided their long tresses.

Villages were located near bayous or lakes and houses were constructed round with walls of a mixture of clay and Spanish moss. Roofs were made of layers of palmetto leaves carefully applied to prevent leakage. Within the village were large thatched "temples" that housed the chief of the tribe. Sentries were constantly on guard against invaders, their stations were lookout towers placed on stilts at outlying positions near the village.

Men of the village were hunters, fishermen and trappers, while the women made gardens of corn, cabbage, wild onions, sweet potatoes, beans, squash and other vegetables. Many of those indians were sophisticated farmers with advanced ideas in tools and implements. Also included in their diet were wild plums, persimmons, grapes, mulberries, strawberries, walnuts, hickory nuts and pecans. Their meat dishes included bear, deer, squirrel, rabbit, turkey and wild fowl, making special meals of fragrant stews and seafood soups.

Louisiana's natural wealth of shell fish, wild birds, animals and plant life was always in abundance and provided constant healthful food supplies during all seasons. When corn was low for making flour the women made bread from ground live oak acorns. They also raised many domesticated animals such as pigs, goats and dogs. In many cases dogs were used as guard protection for the village.

Men hunted birds, animals and fish with spear, blowgun or bow and arrows. Besides farming, women made reed boxes and baskets and cured hides and furs for trading at the market place. From the fat of the bear they produced aromatic oils that were traded to the French and Spanish to use as cosmetic lotions, for hair dressing and for cooking oil. They also crafted such fancy articles as richly beaded turkey feather robes and muskrat mantles for the white man to ship to the courts of France and Spain in exchange for favors granted.

The North American Indian, especially those of the southern tribes, considered themselves above the white colonists in terms of morality, piety and nobility.

Much was learned from the indian way of life; weather protection methods, housing, medicinal plants and roots, herbs for cooking, hunting and trapping practices, transportation and countless survival modes greatly aided the early pioneers and settlers of the Louisiana Territory.

EARLY LOUISIANA FORT

Louisiana's Foremost Settlers

The early eighteenth century brought pronounced changes to areas of southern Louisiana. Native indians began to see strange faces and a new kind of life-way entering their opulent land. Those newcomers were French pioneers from Europe who developed towns and highly productive farms and who became merchants, planters and fishermen. Many of the planters were descendants of nobility from France. Other Frenchmen from the Canadian St. Lawrence Valley settled along the rivers and bayous to become trappers, fishermen and to develop fur trading posts and fishing villages.

Still another group in large numbers were French vagrants and convicts ordered to Louisiana by the King of France to serve as labor forces for French farms and communities. But, it soon became apparent that this human element was not suitable or productive. They were replaced by the more capable and dependable Africans brought into Louisiana as laborers for the fields, for the river front and as servants for the city and plantation homes. Those negroes were very beneficial to the early development of Louisiana. Their ability to withstand prolonged hard work in the hot humid climate proved extremely valuable and their countless contributions have been priceless from the very beginning.

Initially about five hundred negroes were brought to Louisiana to clear the lands for early French pioneers. Eventually, over the years to follow, thousands more were taken over in large and in small groups from the West Indies and from Africa, forming competent work forces for every area of development.

In 1715 noble European Frenchmen founded Louisiana's first town, Natchitoches. Then New Orleans was founded about three years later and the two towns soon developed into important trade centers with essential ports.

But, New Orleans was no different than any other port city, not only did it lure immigrants of honorable nature, but it also atttracted hundreds of undesirables seeking quick and easy money by unsavory methods. There were vagrant seamen from the Caribbean, lowly laborers from France and Cuba and large numbers from the world's oldest profession. Many of them were the scum of flesh peddlers that rose up from the streets and gutters of France, Portugal and Santo Domingo and converged on the streets and gutters of New Orleans. The city became a mixing port of humanity, ranging from royalty down to the lowest gutter rat.

Shortly after the founding of New Orleans many political refugees from Germany settled what is now known as the *German Coast* on the Mississippi River in St. John the Baptist and St. Charles parishes, about thirty miles upriver from New Orleans. They were very poor immigrants who came from the Rhine River Valley and found it very difficult to adjust to the extremely hot humid summers of Louisiana. But, they were strong, healthy and vigorous people who with enthusiastic efforts fought off indians, perpetual floods and the ever present beasts of the swamps to clear the land, build homes, raise vegetables and hunt wild fowl and animals. Many acquired cows from nearby Frenchmen and manufactured dairy products that were sold, together with vegetables and wild fowl, to the markets of New Orleans, bringing those products down river in homemade boats.

Later, more Germans located in New Orleans and smaller towns along the river and bayous to become successful laborers, brewers, shoemakers, metal workers and shopkeepers of many sorts. But, because of the strong French influence already in Louisiana it was not long before those new immigrants had lost their native tongue and had become completely absorbed into the French cultures. Many names presently regarded as French are of German origin: *Leche, Vicknair, Folse, Trosclair, Oubre, Webre, Toups, Himel* and many others are German names with minor alterations in spelling to make them sound more French. But, it should never ever be forgotten that those strong willed and healthy people of German descent with enthusiastic spirits have served in impressive fashion as honorable pioneers of this state. They are strong fibers in the roots of Louisiana.

In 1763 the first Acadians (banished earlier from their homes in Nova Scotia) arrived at the *Acadian Coast* near the present town of Donaldsonville, upriver from the then established *German Coast.* They first settled the Bayou Lafourche areas and many went into Pointe Coupee and Avoyelles parishes. Other Acadians arriving later migrated into the broad lands of the Teche Country. Those new immigrants who were also very poor became small farmers, trappers, fishermen and hunters. Later, many of them moved to the vast southwest Louisiana prairies to become ranchers of wild cattle and farmers....much smaller operations as compared to those planters of large plantations who originally came directly from France.

Many of the Spaniards, Acadians and Frenchmen of the lower Lafourche formed fishing communities in the Barataria Bay area. Other nationalities such as Portuguese and Filipinos who had deserted ships in New Orleans found refuge at these settlements. This mixture of people became known as *"Baratarians"* and harbored hundreds of pirates operating in the Gulf of Mexico. It was those Baratarians, in great numbers, who fought so bravely under Jean Laffite at the Battle of New Orleans.

Some of the poorer French colonists settled along the river in New Orleans working in various shops and on the river front. This group is largely responsible for designing and constructing the ever popular *"shotgun house"* of New Orleans, which was designed for good air circulation and comfort in the humid New Orleans weather.

Much to the surprise and disfavor of the earlier settlers, Spain acquired the Louisiana Territory from France in 1762 and a few years later immigrants from the Canary Islands and mainland Spain began to arrive in Louisiana. The Canary Islanders, known as *"Islenos,"* went in sizeable numbers to Delacroix Island, a few miles southeast of New Orleans, becoming fishermen, trappers and small vegetable farmers. Other Canary Islanders settled fishing communities in the Bayou Lafourche and Bayou Manchac areas.

The immigrants that came from Spain were located in the vicinity of what is presently known as New Iberia. Like the Germans, the Spaniards of Lafourche, Manchac and New Iberia quickly became absorbed by the French and their language; names like *Gomez, Perez, Gonzales, Romero, Martinez, Sanchez* and others soon became Louisiana Frenchmen, speaking French fluently with strong "Cajun" accents, losing their native language completely.

Governing officials and military forces of the Spanish era made their homes in New Orleans. Other than in the areas mentioned above there were very few Spaniards who settled in Louisiana during that period of Spanish rule.

In the year 1800 the French again acquired Louisiana and with the exception of some architecture which has been modified with French overtones, the Spanish contributed very little toward the pioneering advancement of Louisiana. It didn't take long before the early Spanish impression was just about completely removed.

However, the Islenos who settled Delacroix Island have long preserved their language and customs in their own special fashion.

Just a few years before Louisiana was purchased by the United States, British colonial planters from the Carolinas and Virginia moved into the area that is now known as the Feliciana parishes, making cotton and tobacco their main crop. Although they did develop a number of large plantations.....that area was never to compare with the vast and productive empires so prevelent along the Mississippi River between Baton Rouge and New Orleans.

Agricultural booms in cotton early in the nineteenth century brought Anglo-Americans from eastern United States into central and northern Louisiana. The mid-1800's saw completion of the railroad system through the prairies of the southwest making new lands available for open range cattle. Mid-westerners were also attracted to the southwest for corn and rice farming and it was those mid-westerners who are credited with developing rice farming as a major industry in Louisiana. They were of German, Swedish and Danish descent.

In the nineteenth century many new settlers were attracted to the lumber towns of Harvey, Plaquemine, Pontchatoula, Lutcher, Morgan City and Patterson and by 1860 lumbering was very big business in Louisiana. Besides the vast forests of oak, cypress and other hardwoods, pine lumbering covered large areas in the Florida parishes above Lake Ponchartrain and in the Ouachita, Red River and Sabine areas.

In 1830 famine ridden Ireland sent many Irish immigrants to New Orleans. In the beginning those newcomers made up important work crews to dig ditches and canals in and around the city and also formed strong labor forces for heavy construction. Many found work on the river front, at cotton presses, some took over drays and cabs, others became salesmen and some even ventured into politics and private businesses. They established their community along the river in New Orleans, it became popularly known as the *Irish Channel.*

After the Civil War the sugar cane plantations that were still in operation attracted thousands of Italian immigrants to work the fields. They replaced the negroes who had left the plantations during the War. But the Italians were soon proven unsuited for such strenuous prolonged work and were replaced by the negroes who had returned to become hired field workers, sharecroppers and tenants of subdivided land. Italians turned to small vegetable farming and street vending from pushcarts. Many opened oyster, fruit and vegetable stands in New Orleans while Sicilians became farmers and diggers of shellfish, forming new communities along the river just below New Orleans. The terrorist element of the Italians and Sicilians of New Orleans created the organization now known in America today as the *"Mafia."*

New fishing villages were established in the late 1800's by Chinese and Filipino immigrants near and below New Orleans in the Barataria swamps and marsh lands. These were the settlements known as St. Milo and Manilia Villages. Many Chinese and Filipino immigrants had also come to the New World as workers to replace the negroes on plantations. But constant bickering, language barriers and laziness made them worthless for such operations, so they became fishermen, forming their own fishing communities in the Barataria waters.

Slavonian and Dalmation immigrants of the late nineteenth century (nicknamed *"Tacos"* by the Creoles) formed small villages next to the Mississippi River at the lower end of Plaquemines Parish to also become fishermen as well as citrus farmers. Even today their fruit and shellfish stands dot the roadsides of their communities below New Orleans.

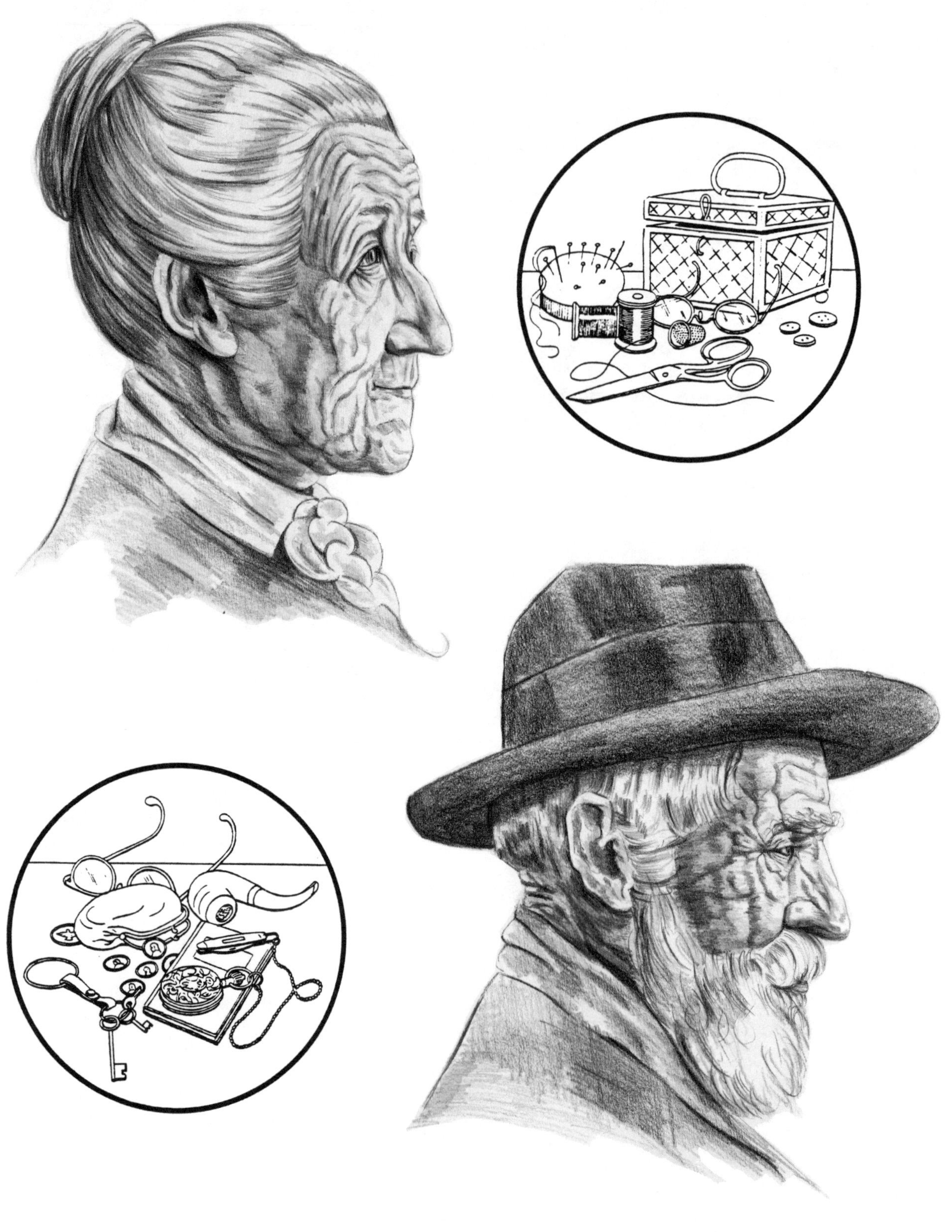

La Grandmère , Le Grandpère

(Tribute to all the elderly Creoles of Louisiana who have given so very much of themselves for future generations.)

There is so much beauty in faces of the old......

Do not erase those lines of so many years that tell me of your life, I want to know and I want to remember.

Sculptured into your face are memories of so much hardship, happiness and love.

Your eyes tell me of the many nights that you were awake with the illness of others. They tell me of the many days of worry when there was little food for the table. They tell me of your prayers of devotion, not for yourself, but for those you held dear to you.

Each line has special significance in memories of your life; grief, worry, peace, love, happiness. The lines beside your eyes tell of the untiring hours of needlework for clothing....or, a squint from too many years of work in blinding sunlight.

I want to remember that devotion to discipline within your household. Reflected in the wrinkles upon your brow are memories of worthy strictness you hated to give; so necessary was it to build a character with respectfulness to all. A discipline so needed for the future, to become a worthy being to mankind.

Do not erase those lines beside your lips that tell me of your joyful loving smiles even during troubled times. Each line, each hair of grey reminds me of your determination and patience.

Keep them there for me and others like me who want to remember how you taught of God and of His need in time of stress; for peace.

All this and so much more I want to remember, for you gave to me a strength and a direction. If I falter and weaken to lesser values of others, I want those memories to awaken me into a decent reality; to tell me of duty to myself, to my fellow man and most of all to my Creator.

I want to be reminded of your ever-struggling efforts of righteousness to others. For I now know that this love, devotion and discipline was not for me alone, but to pass on to others who are in search and in need of a purpose; and, happiness.

Do not remove those sculptured lines or hair of grey for they speak to me so clearly,

And, I want to remember how so very much you have loved.

OAK ALLEY

"No other place can display such a breathtaking beauty to the passerby. It is a living picture that could never have been envisioned by its builder a century and one-half ago. The splendor of those magnificent oaks give great majestic effects yet with such peaceful impressions; all twenty-eight remain today even more beautiful than it had ever hoped they would be.... the soft-shadowed mansion glows beautifully like a pink light at the end of a superbly fashioned emerald tunnel."

PLANTATION VIGNETTES

A LOUISIANA PLANTATION

The Plantation Empire

LAND AND CROP DEVELOPMENT

All along the coast of the Mississippi River from Natchez to New Orleans, in the highlands of the Felicianas, Cane River country, the Bayou Teche basin, on the banks of Bayou Lafourche and at distant isolated country sites there remains many interesting monuments to the yesteryears of the Golden Plantation Era. Some are now private homes, others are public museums, and still others serve as schools or office buildings for business establishments. Many still maintain the prestigious position of being the "main house" of a flourishing modern day plantation, farm or cattle ranch.

Although there have been wide varieties in size and design, all of these remaining memorials are living reminders of Louisiana's heritage. Most of them represent those pioneers who played such an important role during the development of this nation. Plantations of the 1800's shaped the face of the South and Louisiana, transforming forests, marshes and swamplands into prolific rice, tabacco, cotton and sugar cane fields. They nourished the lifebloods of many nations during those formative years.

Each plantation was a village within itself, not only were most of them self-sustaining but they created and supported many other prosperous business ventures throughout the nation. Nowhere on earth were there so many depending on a system that could make for them so much money in such a short period.

In the beginning, the planters established their plantations in somewhat of a meager fashion with very little productivity for national or foreign markets. Emphasis was placed on products needed for local communities; corn, rice, vegetables and meat. Although the land seemed to overproduce vegetation it was difficult to establish a staple crop that would bring in large enough profits to enable them to expand their operations. Many planters tried saffron, hops, myrtle wax, cotton, tobacco and indigo for export profits. For a while tobacco and indigo seemed more profitable, but it wasn't until the discovery of the sugar granulating method and the invention of the cotton gin that plantations were able to rise to the pinnacles of great empires. The successful granulation of sugar detonated the sugar cane industry and the plantation system. This began in the 1790's and by the time of the purchase of Louisiana by the United States in 1803 sugar manufacturing was well on its way to becoming a major industry of this country.

Lowest lands of the state, from central Louisiana south into the bayou areas and along the shores of the lower Mississippi River went to the sugar industry, while the drier upper lands of northern Louisiana and most of the Felicianas went to cotton. By the beginning of the 1800's only about eighty planters raised sugar cane, but within twenty-five years the total had reached to over seven hundred. The number of sugar plantations and the amount of sugar production for export increased steadily for the next thirty years, up until the time of the Civil War.

Rich soils of the Red, Ouachita and Tensas rivers were very suitable for the planting of cotton. With this and the mild climate Louisiana offered opportunities for many planters to well establish themselves at relatively low investments as compared to the large capitals necessary to become a sugar cane planter. It has often been said that it took all the available resources of a wealthy cotton planter to become just a mediocre sugar cane planter. Requirements in the number of workers, factory and harvesting equipment expenses and vast land investments necessitated huge monetary outlays just to begin in the sugar industry. Two unsuccessful sugar cane crops in a row could often be disastrous and perhaps bankrupt the planter, compelling him to sell all of his properties. Many had to do just that and were forced to become small farmers, managers of other plantations or perhaps a shopkeeper in the city.

PLANTATION MASTER (THE PLANTER)

On a successful plantation the owner's life was far from perpetual siestas, mint juleps and "soirees." He could hardly have accomplished much of a degree of success had he been the fabled figure of leisure as tradition frequently depicted in the movies or books of fiction. A successful planter was a very hard worker whose day was long and busy, beginning before sunrise and lasting into the night. Seldom did he enjoy a Sunday of complete leisure and relaxation. There were never ending duties of bookkeeping, purchasing of equipment and supplies, appointments to meet, special business trips and routine supervisory duties. There were many unforeseen emergencies, problems among workers that required personal attention, land developments, social and civic obligations and crop adjustment problems. The plantation owner had to be an economist, an engineer, an effective weather forecaster, a horticulturist and a psychologist. And, he had to be a politician and a statesman in order to effectively engage in successful transactions in the business of selling and shipping of plantation products. He had to be a husband and a father, his family was of ever present interest and concern. The planter had to be proud, compassionate but firm, ambitious, persistent, self-disciplined and a very shrewd business man.

PLANTATION MISTRESS

The planter's wife, the mistress of the "big house," was a person of quite a different character than the "honey tongued" southern plantation woman portrayed in the movies, one who sat around on the verandah all day doing needlepoint and drinking lemonade. The plantation woman was well educated, schooled extensively on management of the household, economics, furnishings, domestic supplies, skills, health care and human relations; she had to be a good manager of personnel affairs. She had to keep herself well informed on styles to teach hairdressers and seamstresses. She taught the servants special skills in the care of clothing, weaving, dying, nursing, cooking and maintenance. She had to be a dietician, medical advisor and counselor. She supervised the negro hospital, presided over all affairs pertaining to the welfare of the servants and was in complete control over operations of the "big house" and its supporting facilities. She often took on many of the duties of her husband when he was away on business trips.

Rising each day before dawn the plantation mistress often found herself engaged in duties far into the night. She managed all social affairs and entertainments for both friends and business guests. Maintaining ample food and medical supplies for the entire plantation was always her responsibility. Because of the ever-present possibility of pilfering of food stocks, supplies and utinsels by the servants it was necessary to keep such supplies under special lock and key. Each pantry or storeroom was unlocked individually by her or a trusted servant to issue necessary provisions.

The mistress arranged services to negro funerals and weddings, attended birthings and illnesses. Often there were several hundred negroes on a single plantation and supervision of their health care was quite an undertaking in itself.

All too often she became a widow early in life and together with the imposing duties already in her care she took over responsibilities of managing the plantation and usually did this as efficiently and as effectively as her husband. Such were the cases of Mary Clara Weeks of the "Shadows-on-the-Teche," Martha Turnbull of "Rosedown," Felicitie Chretien of "Chretien Point," Louise Harvey of "Harvey's Castle" and many others. Yet, in spite of their hardships, trials and responsibilities, reportedly, these women maintained their beauty, femininity and grace as a lady, wife and charming hostess for the numerous gala events of plantation business and social life.

Last, but certainly not the least, the mistress of the plantation was usually a devoted family woman. More often than not she mothered many children, nursing, training and tutoring them until they were old enough to be married. Usually she was their association with the outer world and it was through her that they obtained their education and social exposure.

MANAGERS AND OVERSEERS

Most planters were assisted by either a plantation manager or by an overseer, depending on the magnitude of his holdings. The *MANAGER* held the more prestigious position and although he may not have been a landowner his position in social circles very nearly equalled that of the owner. Other than the owner and his family the plantation manager was the most important and respected figure in plantation society. He was always chosen for his excellent character, good education and management capabilities. He performed many of the duties that most planters performed. He was usually hired by a planter who owned more than one plantation and given full responsibilities as head administrator for one or more plantations. He was awarded a good salary, a nice home well equipped with nice furnishings and his family lived very much in a style familiar to the family of the owner.

An *OVERSEER* was much less in rank than that of the manager and was selected for his abilities to get work forces effectively organized, to create harmony among them and to obtain the greatest amount of efficiency from the workers at his disposal. He selected drivers (straw bosses), maintained disciplines and peace among them and enforced the rules set forth by the planter or manager. He was provided with a comfortable home amply furnished and given an annual salary along with food and clothing allotments. Members of his family were usually privileged with some of the benefits enjoyed by the owners, but hardly ever were they accepted in the same social circles of the owner or manager's family.

LABOR

From the very beginning labor for the plantation had been a very serious problem which wasn't solved until the introduction of the African slaves by the "Company of the West," organized for the specific purpose of transporting slaves into America. African negroes, captured and held in bondage by black African lords, were sold by their black masters to the "Company" on the coast of Africa, then brought over by the shiploads to use for work forces on plantations or in other private businesses throughout the eastern half of the country. Slavery was a far from free labor, it required enormous initial investments and great expenses for annual living provisions, especially pronounced on sugar plantations.

Many of the negroes trained themselves to become skilled workers and achieved prestigious positions. The sugar plantations produced numerous craftsmen: carpenters, blacksmiths, wagon builders, coopers, millwrights, bricklayers, artisians and more. Many household servants distinguished themselves as respected cuisiniers (cooks), coachmen, shoemakers, weavers, seamstresses, nurses and gardeners. Those skilled craftsmen were usually the most intelligent, most ambitious and the most qualified workers who were given special privileges and benefits because of their willingness to improve and perform their skills. Many were accepted as members of the planter's family, especially cooks, nurses, governesses and other servants of the household. Quarters for these special workers were near the main house and not in the field village.

The negro village consisted of numerous cabins for housing, a church and a community kitchen. There was also a plantation store and a hospital to serve their needs. Field workers and unskilled laborers lived in the village. Care for young children was a responsibility given to elderly negroes who were too old to perform laborious duties.

Most of the plantation owners allowed each negro family to raise private vegetable gardens and to have poultry and hogs that could be used in supplement to regular provisions furnished to them by the planter. Many of them sold vegetables and chickens to traveling tradesmen so that they could purchase extras such as Sunday clothing, liquor, etc. Often the skilled and the most assiduous workers were able to save enough from their earnings to buy their way out of bondage to become free and independent business people, many with plantations and slaves of their own.

The field workers planted, cultivated and harvested crops, worked the sugar mills, sawmills, cotton gins and presses. Construction materials for housing and other buildings were made from timber taken from nearby forests and finished into lumber, roofing shingles, fencing materials, etc. On some plantations the sugarhouse, the negro cabins and the main house were all constructed with bricks made right on the plantation. But, most negroes objected to this construction believing that bricks harbored evil spirits that gave them the "miseries" (illnesses).

"Work gangs" of men and women maintained levees and roads, cleaned ditches and repaired fences. Men cut firewood for mill operations and for home heating and cooking. Hundreds of cords of wood were required annually for that purpose. Each gang of twenty or less workers were supervised by a ***driver*** who was chosen for their ability to get others to work steadily and without conflict. On most plantations, hard physical labor for heavy construction (building levees, digging canals and ditches, etc.) was done by white workers, usually Irish labor forces who roamed the country in gangs performing work of that nature for a fee paid by the planter. Most plantation owners did not risk the health and life of the negroes by imposing too strenuous and dangerous work on them. The negro was too valuable to them for working the crops and other operational jobs. Work on the plantation was never ending, but the most demanding of southern agricultural labor was the harvesting of sugar cane crops, a season that lasted from October through December. There were also numerous other work loads necessary for a successful plantation; corn, hay, fodder, peas and other crop cultivating and harvesting.

Because of the ever present exposure to bad weather, industrial accidents and wildlife menaces, personal traumas and tragic events were more frequent and more intimately related than in other communities. With so many people in such closely knitted hamlets everyone felt the sorrows of the others. Families were much larger and the members closer to one another, with many of the negroes often regarded as part of the family. Even distant field workers were looked upon with more compassion when it came to personal misfortunes. Serious illnesses, accidents and deaths effected everyone in a very special way.

Depending upon policies set by individual planters, negro entertainments varied from one plantation to the other. Many planters allowed their workers recreational privileges to a generous degree as long as it did not interfere with their work performance or with the peace and efficiency of their neighbor. There were negro church socials, batture night parties and many of the white entertainments included the negroes, such as traveling showboats and horse racing at neighboring plantations. Fishing and hunting of wild animals and birds in nearby forests were common enjoyable pastimes. Following sugar cane grinding and during the Christmas season were favorite times of the year for the negroes, their parties were frequent and in festive fashion.

CHILDREN OF THE PLANTATION

From the cradle until marriage the *planter's children* were under the constant supervision of their parents. Although most of them were placed in the care of a governess and tutors, their parents maintained strict rule over their conduct, training and social life. Many of them had selected negro playmate at an early age and often those relationships molded close friendships that lasted throughout their lifetime.

Private tutors were engaged to teach the young people of the planter's family all the essential subjects; reading, writing, arithmetic, geography, English, music, dancing and painting. When old enough, many of them received further education at convents and colleges such as Sacred Heart Academy or St. Charles and Jefferson Colleges. Often sons of Creoles were sent to Paris for higher education and some of the young ladies of American families received advanced schooling in South Carolina and Virginia.

Young people of the plantations were very active in entertainments and when not in school they were kept quite busy; music, reading painting, sewing, lawn parties, sugarhouse parties, hayrides, horseback riding, boating, hunting, and fishing were just some of their recreations. Many included young people from nearby plantations. Occasionally they vacationed in Europe with friends or relatives and frequently traveled with parents to New Orleans, Natchez or other cities to attend the theatre or opera.

Most of them followed in the footsteps of their parents by becoming the master or mistress of their own plantation, either by inheritance, marriage or by purchasing their own land. There were, however, some young men who became lawyers, merchants and doctors, and occasionally young plantation women married men of professions other than in agriculture to venture into entirely different lifestyles than that of their parents.

Negro children received limited schooling, but on some plantations schoolhouses were built and teachers hired for the purpose of teaching negro children reading, writing and other minor subjects.

There were work programs for negro children designed specifically to teach them responsibilities and discipline. Elderly negro men and women supervised those groups whose duties were picking up trash, weeding gardens, performing chores for household servants, attending to the poultry and livestock and running errands.

MAIN HOUSE DESIGN

Early plantation houses in Louisiana were frame cottages raised above the ground by brick pillars to various heights depending upon the land flooding possibilities in the area. The *Creole cottage* and the *Louisiana Colonial* house, which was patterned with some features taken from the West Indies style plantation house, were architectural expressions unique to Louisiana and to the Creole standards of living. Those standards were inherited from French province lifestyles rather than from the American designs of eastern states that reflected English codes. Although the early Creole and Louisiana Colonial house may appear smaller and less spectacular than the massive mansions of Louisiana Greek Revival of later years, they were by no means any less important to the plantation system and to the development of Louisiana.

French Creoles were a product of Louisiana soils, to them living was an art styled for specific purposes of family and religion. Their homes were designed for the maximum of comfort at the minimum of expense. It was a very practical design in a land of mild winters and long hot humid summers. Everything on the Creole plantation was planned and executed with one thought in mind; the needs and comforts of every individual who lived on the plantation. The home meant far more to them than it did to the city dweller.

To the plantation family the home was a place where many of them spent their entire life. They were born in it, reared in it, they were taught school in it, were married in it, raised their own family there and died in it. It was a business establishment, it was a social center and a place for visitors to enjoy. It was a place of recreation, a place for their religious services and a school for the young.

The Creole cottage and the Louisiana Colonial houses were designed to make every square foot of space usable and practical. Huge rooms with high ceilings, large shuttered windows and doors and spacious galleries created cool refreshing atmospheres for pleasant living during the summer months. Bousillage walls and fireplaces warmed the rooms in comfort during the winter time. Central hallways were seldom included and most of the rooms opened directly unto the galleries. High and dormered gable roofs offered additional space in attics to make loom and weaving rooms or quarters for the young men of the family.

Kitchens, smokehouses, laundry rooms and other service buildings were often built detached from the main house for reasons of protection against fire and to avoid disturbing noises or odors. And always, a place in the home was reserved for a private chapel for religious services. The Creole home reflected warm atmospheres of a closely knitted religious French family. Large or small, it was almost never any more or any less than what was required to serve the family, guests and plantation management needs. Hospitality was superb, food was excellent and plentiful and living was comfortably serene.

Louisiana Classic designs were modifications of the Louisiana Colonial with Greek Revival overtones. The wide galleries, spacious rooms and steep roofs were retained, but massive columns running from the ground to the roof and wide hallways were introduced, outside stairs were moved to the interior. More expensive and elaborate furnishings replaced modest pieces; parlors and dining areas expanded. However, warm intimate atmoshperes were retained and personable friendly environments of the Creoles seemed enriched by those elegant additions.

The migration of Americans to Louisiana during the early 1800's brought into the Louisiana plantation system a *Greek Revival* craze which was obviously intended for colossal effects; great houses fronted by massive columns were without galleries, large windows and spacious doors. Flanking the main house were smaller reproductions used for offices, guest cottages, garconniers and the use of pigeonnieres were adopted from the Creoles. Even though the designs were more imposing than the earlier Creole homes they reflected more formal and impersonal attitudes and lifestyles. Larger than necessary hallways and stairways; ballrooms, music rooms and libraries became the fashion, but family rooms and work areas appeared more confining and less comfortable. These homes, although quite impressive to the outsider, projected a standoffish appearance sharply contrasting the warm inviting atmospheres of the early Louisiana homes.

On all plantations, acreages surrounding the main house yielded explosions of foliage; beautiful flowering shrubs, hedges, roses, camelias, magnolias and great live oaks were everywhere. Formal gardens became fashionable and spacious vegetables gardens, fruit and nut orchards and children's playgrounds were the custom. Stables, barns, workshops, poultry and livestock yards, terrapin ponds and man-made lakes were necessary fundamental components of the plantation.

CONCLUSION

The plantation was a *Manufacturing Establishment* that created products to aid the requirements of mankind. The plantation was a *Settlement Establishment* with the big house as a center for activity, serving as the headquarters for a complete community of working people; skilled tradesmen, laborers, shops and equipment. The plantation was an *Economic Establishment;* it was to the large city what the small farm was to the village or town. It stimulated economies by creating businesses and jobs needed to transport products, to furnish equipment and replenish supplies for supporting establishments. The plantation was a *Political Establishment* that operated with a high degree of consistency, setting up strict laws and governing rules for necessary efficiency. The plantation was a *Cultural Establishment* that provided a way of life common to everyone and was controlled by its own code of ethics.

The Louisiana plantation was a *Monumental Establishment* of America, a major industry that served people of all nations for many generations. It was an institution of proud people that have made indelible impressions upon Louisianians and have become perpetual reminders of the unparalleled achievements of their pioneering ancestors.

DeHart

Memories Cast In Silver

The voice of the great plantation
was the ringing of the bell,
It told of sickness, it told of death
and it tolled when all was well.

It sent workers into the field
at the beginning of each day,
And brought them home at night
in a tired and weary way.

It tolled the Angelus each morning
it rang at noon and nightly,
To announce a time for prayer
giving thanks to God Almighty.

It rang for church on Sunday
and to stir the young for school,
To make ready for a wedding
as a cheerful beckoning tool.

There was never a new born baby
to come upon this earth,
Who wasn't greeted with chimes
for announcements of its birth.

It sang out so very cheerfully
news of an on-coming guest,
Or knelled a word of sadness
when a soul was laid to rest.

It often pealed out warnings
of a devastating flood,
And summoned all hands to help
to fill a crevasse with mud.

It may have tolled for raging fires
on cold wintry nights,
Or of coming summer storms
that brought on fearful flights.

Continued . . . . . .

It sang out chimes of joy
of old fashion Christmas Seasons,
Or sent out gleeful messages
for so many other reasons.

Let's join together to pay tribute
to this loyal and noble servant,
The silver toned Plantation Bell
that served so well with fervent.

It may sit there now in silence
upon a trestled tower,
But let us ne'er forget
its one time revered power.

Perils of Ormond

On the east bank of the Mississippi River just about a mile and a half north of the famed Destrehan plantation home the traveler will come upon another Louisiana historical gem. This attractive old home; erected in the 1790's, has been plagued with tragic events and sadness almost from the very day of her creation.

She has witnessed sad mysteries, violent deaths, disastrous crop failures and unexpected fatal illnesses; leaving one to truly believe that only fate could have imposed such curses upon land and dwelling.

The mournful events that have surrounded "Ormond" have spoken out in silent persistence showing a deterioration that seems to resist all faithful efforts to keep the old home rejuvenated. Her ancient weathered cypress columns, her powdering sun-baked bricks and her flaking stucco walls seemed to constantly defy any effort to restore her to her original beauty. Still, she stood there in secluded loneliness appearing to beckon to anyone who may want to grant to her a compassion that will extend her life with an understanding mankind. Her summoning aura has produced hypnotic influences upon those with a concern for her wellbeing.

Ormond's builder and master, Pierre Trepagnier, a Frenchman of nobility, had honorably distinguished himself in defense of Louisiana when Governor Bernardo de Galvez and his forces successfully defeated the British in 1789. Those noble efforts of Pierre Trepagnier were rewarded with vast land grants that extended from the Mississippi River to Lake Ponchartrain. On this land he built his home and became a successful planter.

Pierre was to live with his creation for only a few short years before his mysterious disappearance which was never explained or never solved.....one morning in 1798 he had just sat down to breakfast with his family of eight when a stranger rode up on horseback and asked a servant if he could speak with the master of the house. After a brief conversation with the stranger, Pierre returned to tell his family that he must go on an errand but would return to them in a short while; he left on horseback with the caller. He was never again seen or never again heard from.

A year later, after many anxious months of unbearable nights waiting for him to return, his bereaved wife exhausted with grief abandoned Ormond, taking her children with her. Sad years followed for the once loved and cared for mansion.

In 1812 Richard Butler, (an ex-officer in the Revolutionary Army with Marquis de Lafayette) bought Ormond and became a gentleman planter, bringing his new bride (daughter of the Spanish Governor of Natchez) to make their home in this riverside manor. His fortunes grew in just a few short years and for a while their marriage was a happy one, even without children. Then, one disaster was followed by another; bad crops, floods, storms and finally a yellow fever epidemic that claimed the lives of both Butler and his young wife. It was this couple that gave the present name of "Ormond" to this grand dwelling. They had named it after one of Richard's relatives who had been the Earl of Ormond.

Once more the plantation fell suddenly into quietness and soon began to show signs of weariness and age. But, again it was saved, this time by a friend of Richard Butler. A sea captain by the name of Samuel McCutchon purchased Ormond from Butler's relatives. He then married one of Butler's sisters, became a planter and installed new life into the old mansion with nine children in rapid succession. Year after year, there were many grand crops and he had great successes as a planter.

The McCutchons added the twin wing garconnieres to accommodate a flourishing family with high spirits. Ormond gleamed again in rich yellows and whites with matching colors for negro cabins. The old girl was again dressed in fineries imported from England, France and Italy. For a time there was much good fortune and splendor at Ormond.

Then, as before, bad times began to appear in the guise of flood waters, devastating storms and deaths along with the grief, misery and ruinations brought on by the Civil War. Ormond sank once again into a period of sadness and slow decay. One by one members of the family left for distant places, others passed away and finally the old home became encompassed by the same loneliness it had been so accustomed to over past years.

Late during the 1890's a family by the name of LaPlace rescued her from ruins and for a short time Ormond was again prosperous, peaceful and joyous. Then, history repeated itself and tragedy struck in almost the exact same fashion as once before. One night while seated peacefully at the supper table with his family Mr. LaPlace was visited by a strange caller. He left the house on what his wife said was a routine short errand: he never returned to his supper; he never returned to his family that night. On the following morning his bullet riddled body was found hanging by a rope from the great oak that shades the front yard. As it had happened before, this mysterious crime was never solved. Again, Ormond was abandoned to nature's destructive elements.

An old negro man and his wife brought temporary hope to Ormond as tenants to this magnificent manor. But, the task was too great and too tiring for those with weary bones. Restoration and even normal maintenance efforts were fruitless for this aging couple. They too were forced to desert Ormond and for years she lay there alone, tired and sad, without a friend, without hopes.

In recent years, before Ormond had completely sunk into obliteration she was again rescued and beautifully restored with a new life, new colors and new furnishings. Ormond stands today in a grand and noble fashion amid tranquil shades of the stately old trees that embelish her spacious grounds. She is a splendidly preserved relic of the bygone days of Louisiana plantation life. But.....how long will it be before the present day traveler will again begin to detect flaking paint, crumbling mortar and powdering bricks? Will those signs of sadness again begin to reappear?

Could the cursed spirits of damnation that may have occurred centuries ago have been trapped within the walls during the construction of Ormond? Could the sacred grounds of an ancient indian nation have been invaded and sacrilegiously desecrated, bringing a curse to any or all who may dwell within? Will these spirits continue a perpetual restlessness that will over and over again bring sorrow and trauma within those bounds?.....What tragic events still lurk in the shadows of the great oaks or behind the ancient walls waiting to defy those who may want to preserve Ormond's beauty for future generations to enjoy?.....Yes, other manors have suffered recessions, misfortunes and unhappiness as well as successes and gaiety, but very few have experienced so many troubled periods with such ill fortunes and sadness.

Still.....what makes Ormond so special that in spite of almost inevitable annihilation she always seems to have another patron waiting to rescue her and give her just one more chance? Will those haunting, revolting and persistent spirits eventually win out and bring about her total destruction? Or, will those spirits finally give in to tranquility, happiness and longevity to a patient and deserving master; after time and understanding has pacified them into everlasting contentment?

BELLE ALLIANCE

INGLESIDE

J DeHart

Harvey's Castle

A mansion for royalty is what Captain Joseph Hale Harvey built for his lovely wife Louise. It was a landmark of a genius who built it for "his queen" with non-slave labor in the unbelievable period of only ninety days.

In 1845, acting as his own architect, he constructed this mansion on the canal across the river from New Orleans; having eleven enormous rooms, spacious halls and ceilings reaching in heights of eighteen feet.

The Captain and his bride of silks presided over this grandeur and from balconies of the towers they enjoyed breathtaking panoramic views of the canal traveled by hundreds from industries of timber, citrus, vegetable, fur, indigo and Indian traders who rode the waters to and from New Orleans.

His "queen" reigned in elegance over this lavish household and guests came from everywhere to behold and indulge in the fabulous romantic settings of "Harvey's Castle." Queen Louise was every bit her title as she gracefully adorned the halls and gardens of this grand domicile.

Adjoining the grounds of the Castle was a gallery of fine paintings and art treasures brought into the Harvey domain for all, rich or poor, to enjoy. The young were schooled on the values of appreciating fine art pieces.

When business receipts declined after the Captain's death, Louise rose to new pinnacles of achievements by conducting her husband's affairs with such great results that she was once again proclaimed "Queen of the Canal," in different fashion.

She completed the canal locks her husband had begun and was successful overseer to all operations until her death at nearly eighty years of age.

A son, Horace Hale Harvey, assumed the Castle and canal operations, but through neglect this grand old mansion quickly became the victim of decay and in 1924 the Federal Government demolished it when Harvey Canal was purchased for a public waterway.

Harvey's Castle had died, but everlasting memories will remain of this fascinating, romantic and prosperous kingdom that became a reality because of the devoted love of a sea captain for this beautiful maiden of the d'Estrehans;

"his Queen," Louise.

J DeHart

"Misty"

Scores of riverboat travelers told delightful stories of watching this tiny lovely maiden race her magnificent stallion against great paddle boats; thunderous hooves pounding like monstrous drums upon the green shoulders of the great Mississippi.

Bareback upon her handsome steed she'd glide ever so gracefully over levees and pastures along the river's shores. Sprinkled with gold dust her long silken tresses glistened in the sunlight as they brushed wildly over her naked shoulders.

She emitted auras of joy and love, ever so radiant she was of celestial beauty. Mild breezes were sweetened generously by her voice in song and meadows of flowers smiled happily at her presence; she breathed new life into the countrysides.

So suddenly she would appear, only in areas of genuine peace. Then, just as quickly she'd vanish leaving delightful fragrances in the air. Because of her, the birds sang sweeter, flowers bloomed prettier and frigid hearts were generously blessed with warmth.

Visions of this lovely little lady were seen only in those tranquil hours shortly after dawn when the dew had freshly touched the earth and when the sun's rays were still kind to such fragile maidens. She relished all moments of nature's gentleness.

Her dream-like angelic-beauty gave cause to name her *"Misty"* and plantation negroes with widened eyes and affectionate tones spoke of her as *'Missy Angel' returning to earth from the heavens in search of the lover she had left behind.*

Whether this beautiful maiden is a mythical being....many minds do differ. But, in early morn when the sun is gentle and the dewdrops glisten with wetness, some still say this lovely goddess, bathed so beautifully in heavenly mist, can be seen astride her splendid mount roaming the peaceful emerald meadows near Evergreen plantation.

NOTTOWAY

Nottoway

John Hampden Randolph, a native of Virginia, was raised in Woodville, Mississippi, where as a young man he was taught dancing, painting and dueling by John James Audubon. Young Randolph was handsome, six feet tall, blonde hair, blue eyes and with a physique well proportioned to his height. He was the son of Judge Peter Randolph, a planter who had moved his family from Virginia to Mississippi in 1820.

At the age of nineteen John married Emily Jane Liddell, daughter of a wealthy cotton planter of Mississippi. Her dowery was twenty slaves and $20,000.00, extended to her by her father. Following the death of his father in 1841 John bought new land in Louisiana and after a few years there as a cotton planter he mortgaged his property, borrowed more money from his father-in-law and made investments to become a sugar cane planter. His Forest Home plantation in St. James Parish slowly began to show profits and he was soon on his way toward becoming successful as a sugar cane planter. The original home of four rooms soon began to take on new dimensions, as his family grew he added more rooms to the house. In 1857, with eleven children, three boys and eight girls he decided it was time to build a new and larger home to better accommodate his large family.

He hired the famed architect Henry Howard and made plans for an elaborate home that would face the Mississippi River on new land he had purchased for the expansion of Forest Home plantation. It would be the finest home in Louisiana, nothing was too good for his family, especially for his daughters. By 1859 that dream became a splendid reality of fifty rooms and he named it Nottoway, after his native county in Virginia.

When completed Nottoway was a massive and impressive structure and was everything John Randolph had wanted for his family. Two main stories stood above a sizable basement which was brick covered with white stucco. The twenty-two unusually slender columns fronted two story galleries that were crowned with ornate cast-iron handrails. Two matching sets of gray granite entrance steps curved gracefully at each side of the first floor gallery. There were two hundred windows in the house and six stairways.

On the roof sat two rainwater cisterns with a total capacity of 10,000 gallons which furnished water for the entire household, including two indoor bathrooms; one of the first homes of the south to install modern bathrooms with piped-in water. For wintertime heating of the water, copper pipes ran from the cisterns through the fireplaces and furnished hot running water for bathing and washing.

Of the fifty rooms, twelve of them had Carrara marble mantels fronting the fireplaces. Two elegantly furnished parlors with removable partitions opened into one mangificent room known as the "White Ballroom." With the exception of one daughter who had died at an early age, all the Randolph girls were married in this grand ballroom.

The splendid dining room, elaborately furnished with hand-carved furniture, measured twenty-five feet wide and thirty-five feet long. Hallways were twenty feet in width and high-backed chairs and mammoth sofas outlined them, while fine oil paintings graced the white plastered walls.

French ornaments dressed Italian marble mantels and beautiful toilet sets adorned the tops of splendidly carved commodes and bureaus. On every floor in every room there were rich carpets from Europe and Asia. Heavy silk damask drapes matched designs and textures of those on chairs and four-poster bed canopies.

For lighting purposes, a private plant manufactured gas from coal shipped to Nottoway by riverboat. There were culinary departments, sewing rooms, laundry rooms, house servant quarters, wine cellars and storage pantries of every kind. There were separate quarters for the boys and private suites for the girls. The many frequent guests that came to visit Nottoway were taxied to and from steamboat landings in masterfully crafted carriages drawn with elegantly groomed horses. (During those early days the river was much further away than it is today, having changed its course considerably since the 1800's).

Upon approaching Nottoway from the river, there was a stately iron gate for carriages flanked by two smaller pedestrian gates which opened onto a roadway lined with catalpa and magnolia trees. The road wound leisurely through a front pasture where sheep and cattle grazed, and on toward the mansion. About halfway to the house was a fence of hawthorne hedge and another gate that opened unto a poplar lined avenue that ended at a circled drive in front of the house entrance.

Within the circle was a meandering walkway lined with jasmines and other low flowering shrubs. A gazebo stood on the right of the avenue near the circle and a greenhouse was midway between the house and the hawthorne hedge.

At a distance to the right of the house were many great oaks and a screen of shade trees separating the overseers home from the main house. In the overseers yard stood a large tower topped by a plantation bell. Behind that house at some distance was a negro village built in a square with private streets. Several dozen cabins neatly surrounded a large low building used for community gatherings and a nursery for children of working negroes. A special kitchen for cooking meals for the field workers stood at the edge of the village and a church, cemetery and hospital was located at two opposite corners of the community.

At the left front, facing the main house was an ancient indian mound with a shrub lined walkway meandering over its top, descending with steps near the hawthorne fence. A man-made lake stocked with fish offered a playground for ducks, geese and swans. In the center of the lake was a tiny island with a gazebo and small boats were always handy for leisure boating or fishing.

A childrens playground and schoolhouse bordered the south side of the house with an orchard of fruit and nut at the edge of it. To the rear of the playground, separated by trees, were carriage houses, hutches, sheds, chicken yards and stables. Beyond all this lay vegetable gardens and a terrapin pond. Both the pond and the front lake were formed by the removal of clay for the making of bricks for construction of the house.

At a distance to the rear and at the center of the fields Randolph had built his mill to process the three thousand acres of sugar cane. In addition to this there were several thousand acres of woodland and swamp for lumber and hunting wild game. Between the cane fields and swampland he had laid out a "bearfield," which was a border of corn fields grown especially to lure wild animals and birds away from the gardens, orchards and livestock.

The plantation had many skilled craftsmen and workers; cooks, carpenters, bricklayers, plasterers, mechanics, blacksmiths, seamstresses, nurses, teachers and many others. Nottoway had five hundred negro slaves who kept the plantation in top working condition twelve months of the year.

Prior to the Civil War it became one of the best furnished and perhaps the most self-sustaining plantation in the country. Very few others rivaled it in luxury. Negroes at Nottoway were far more comfortable than many "well-to-do" white people of the old country.

The home was spared from shelling during the Civil War by a Union officer who had been friendly with the Randolphs and on several occasions prior to the War had been a guest to their home. The opulent times diminished after the War, but the Randolphs did manage to live in comfort in spite of the adverse and distasteful conditions that followed.

John Hampden Randolph died in 1889 and shortly after Mrs. Randolph was forced to sell the majestic structure with all its furnishings for a mere $100,000.00. Before leaving, the bereaved widow in black walked through the entire home making certain that every one of its two hundred windows were shut and locked. She walked slowly through her beloved White Ballroom and with tears in her eyes she unwillingly descended the gray granite steps. Without turning back, even for one last look, she entered the carriage that brought her to a waiting riverboat. She had enjoyed her lovely "White Castle" for only thirty short years, but as she departed Emily Jane Randolph took with her more beautiful memories than most people can gather during an entire lifetime.

INDIAN CAMP

Indian Camp

According to a map drawn by Adrienne Persac in 1858 (commonly called "Norman's Chart"), the plantation was first named "Woodlawn." The manor house was built in 1857 for R. C. Camp, owner of the plantation at Point Clair, located twenty-five miles south of Baton Rouge on the east shores of the Mississippi River. It is on land that was once the site of an old Houmas Indian village. There are strong indications that the house was designed by the famous architect Henry Howard, the same architect that designed Nottoway, Madewood and many other nineteenth century Louisiana homes.

Although there is very little known about this plantation prior to 1894, what is so important about Indian Camp is that the old home, its slave cabins and supporting buildings on three hundred thirty-seven acres of land played a very unique role in creating a very special health facility for America. It is now the U. S. Public Health Hospital for the treatment of Hansen's disease.

Hansen's disease (leprosy as it was first called) was one of the most dreaded diseases known to man. Today, due to the great advancements made in research and treatment at the hospital at Indian Camp, the disease is no longer so greatly feared and patients of today are not considered to be a threat to society as they once were years ago.

Lepers in early Louisiana were first confined to the island of Balize near the mouth of the Mississippi to live out a life of terror in the mosquito and reptile infested marshes. When Governor Miro came into power he condemned that location as being inhumane and had the lepers moved to a new site on Bayou St. John, just north of New Orleans, where they could be better taken care of. That new area became known as La Terre des Lepreux (Leper's Land) and the infirmary was named the "Hospital for Infectious Diseases."

In the latter part of the 1800's a young seventeen year old cub reporter for the New Orleans Picayune newspaper by the name of John Kendall Smith visited the hospital and in anger wrote a series of articles condemning the facility, calling it "unsanitary, shamefully dirty and in a very deplorable condition." His articles stirred such great controversy and adverse publicity for politicians that the State Legislature created a Board of Controls to locate and to fund a new home for the leper patients of Louisiana.

The only site obtainable for a hospital was the old abandoned Indian Camp plantation at Point Clair. The state obtained the plantation with its deteriorating mansion, slave cabins, supporting structures and three hundred thirty-seven acres of its land.

But, when the patients were moved from the New Orleans hospital to the plantation, nurses could not be found to attend to them. When news of this came out the Daughters of Charity of St. Vincent dePaul, a Roman Catholic Order of nuns from the Provincial House of Emmitsburg, Maryland, volunteered to serve at the hospital. Four of them were chosen and with Sister Beatrice Hart of Boston in charge they were sent to Indian Camp.

Problems were plentiful for the nuns with a run-down mansion with its bad roof, broken windows and missing doors. Rats, snakes, bats and other freightful creatures had occupied the buildings and the marshy land covered with dense weeds harbored millions of dreadful mosquitoes. But, the nuns immediately went to work and with the help of the leper patients they cleared the land, repaired buildings and made vegetable gardens. Cabins were repaired for housing the patients and the "main house" was converted into an infirmary, administration facility and dormitory for the nuns. With the assistance of state funds they began their long, hard struggle to convert that old abandoned plantation into one of the finest public health hospitals in the entire country. Those efforts were to later be greatly rewarded.

Sister Beatrice died in 1901 of malaria but due to her hard work and persistence the buildings were completely renovated and modernization of all facilities took place in 1906. By 1914 the hospital had a modern fresh water system and telephone service.

Accomplishments by Dr. Isadore Dyer, who discovered the treatment for leprosy, and by the Sisters of Charity were so successful and distinguished that in 1921 the Federal Government purchased the entire system from the state. All of the operations were assigned to the United States Public Health Service. The hospital became the only one of its kind in the entire nation for the treatment of Hansen's disease.

Existing today on those same three hundred thirty-seven acres of land is a large complex of one hundred buildings and recreational facilities. There is an infirmary, school facility, church with two chaplains, private residences for the staff, private homes and quarters for the patients, an eighteen hole golf course, swimming pool, tennis courts, twenty acre Lake Johansen for fishing and boating, indoor recreational equipment, a theatre, service buildings and the finest medical facilities and care as can be found anywhere. There is also a printing office, a canteen, a U. S. Post Office, library and auditorium. There are rehabilitation programs for patients, occupational therapy units and manual arts shops for patient enterprises.

Fronting this entire system of buildings and land is that very same plantation manor house where this all started in 1894. Beautifully renovated and preserved, this fine old Louisiana Classic home still serves as the administration building for this hospital. Members of the hospital staff are commissioned officers of the United States and Career Federal Civil Service employees. In this service are twenty or more Sisters of Charity who are registered nurses with B. S. degrees. There are also nuns who provide services in the capacity of registered pharmacists, medical librarians, dieticians and x-ray technologists.

From its very beginning in 1894 until today, the Sisters of Charity have played essential roles in the founding and operating of this very important hospital on the old Indian Camp plantation.

J DeHart

"La Cuisiniere"

That special gift to the planter's household
ever so dependable and true,
She could cook a meal for any king
t'was nothing she could not do.

Recipes were stored in her head
handy for her to create,
In that Beehive oven or roasting mill
or a pan set over the grate.

Forever busy from dawn to dusk
with delights in every pot,
She'd grind and roast and brew up a storm
there was nothing that she'd forgot.

She was the great little wizard of the kitchen
and a magical wand she'd wave,
To arouse those sleeping taste buds
every one of her dishes they'd crave.

Her biscuits were more than special
with butter and coffee or milk,
And French breads or corn meal fritters
in the mouth they'd quickly melt.

Many of her dishes were brought over
from the west African lands,
And there were those she concocted herself
with her own creative hands.

There were delicious soups and filé gumbos
with shellfish, okra and peas,
And her jambalayas and chicken stews
and desserts that were sure to please.

Everyone loved her, 'specially little boys
who'd sneak in to taste her stew,
Or her puddings, or her pies, or her cakes
or, "here's som'pin jus fo you!"

Continued . . . .

He'd run her errands with much delight
for he knew she'd have for him,
An apple puff or a lemon tart, or
candy goodies on a stem.

Not enough can be said of her skills
and her nature was jolly and kind,
But often she'd have to get firm
just to keep those young 'uns in line.

Not just boss of the plantation kitchen,
her domain extended afar,
To gardens, smokehouse, storage and lockers
with specialities stored in a jar.

She ruled with the wisdom of a queen
very selective and sometimes gallant,
And made sure she had the best
to produce the gifts of her talent.

She will be remembered quite well
by those who can still recall,
And history books should tell to others
the joys she gave to them all.

Shadows·On·The·Teche

A very appropriate monument to the memory of a man of enormous stature. David Weeks was the son of William Weeks, a wealthy Englishman who had come to settle in Louisiana's Feliciana country. William also acquired vast amounts of acreage in the Teche country and sent his seven foot tall son, David, to develop that land. David's accomplishments soon became as impressive as his physical stature. He built a sugar cane and cotton empire of seven plantations, totalling 10,000 acres. He named them: Parce Perdu, Cypremort, Shell Mound, Alice, Acadie, Richohoc, Town Farm and Weeks Island. In 1831 their new home on the west bank of the ancient Bayou Teche was completed. His wife, Mary Clara, planted beautiful gardens with numerous trees and plants and they named their new haven *"Shadows-On-The-Teche."*

David died unexpectedly in 1834 while on a business trip in Connecticut and for the thirty years to follow Mary Clara continued to manage the plantations as efficiently and as effectively as her husband had.

As it was with so many of the antebellum mansions, their home was used by Federal troops during the Civil War; the "Shadows" served as the headquarters for the Union Army General Nathanial Banks. Upon this occupancy Mrs. Weeks retired to the upstairs portion of the home, never again to set foot downstairs. She died during the occupation by Federal soldiers; some said that she succumbed to hunger, while others asserted that she had died of a broken heart and humiliation.

After the War, their son William took over management of the home and plantations. William had two daughters; Pattee, who became Mrs. Walter Torian of New Orleans and Lily who married Major Gilbert Hall of New York. Major Hall was a Yankee defector during the War and had become an officer in the Confederate Army. Living at the Shadows with her father they too eventually became managers of the estate.

Gilbert and Lily had only one child, a son, and they named him Weeks Hall. He was a very talented artist and received a scholarship to the Pennsylvania Academy of Fine Arts. During World War I Weeks served in the Office of Naval Intelligence and when the war ended he went to France to further his career in art. He became a free ranging individual who was as much at home on the Seine as he was on the Teche and for years worked as a successful artist in Paris. He liked Parisians, most of his friends were peasants, fishermen, merchants, artists and cabaret singers and dancers. He loved plain people, Frenchmen and Americans alike. Weeks remained a bachelor throughout his entire life.

When Weeks Hall returned to the Techeland in 1922 he set about with the task of restoring the badly neglected grand old homestead to its original status. Thanks to his great-grandfather, David, he was receiving a lucretive income of royalties from the salt mines of Weeks Island, allowing him to live comfortably at the Shadows for the next thirty-nine years. Although he remained a bachelor his life was not a lonely one, besides his paintings he had many friends and visitors; writers, artists, journalists, actors and other notable personalities were forever visiting him. Many have written of their enjoyable memories at the Shadows with Weeks and his friends.

One great fear that Weeks Hall constantly nursed was the fact that perhaps after his death the Shadows could be destroyed for the sake of "progress," to make room for a parking lot or a building of inferior modern architecture. It was because of this fear of its abuse or destruction that at his death in 1961 he bequeathed the home and its grounds to the National Trust for Historic Preservation. It has since been declared a National Historic Landmark by the Department of Interior, thus becoming a lasting memorial to two imposing figures of Louisiana history, David and Mary Clara Weeks.

Still remaining today are many of the furnishings and treasures of the family and the Weeks Hall Studio has been kept in tact, just as it was when he used it daily to create his many paintings, some of them still preserved within the old home.

The Renoudet Cottage, presently at 315 East Saint Peter Street, was built in 1830 and used as the home for the David Weeks plantation's business manager. It is perhaps the oldest frame house standing on its original site in New Iberia.

This rose colored gem, constructed with handmade bricks, glows from within a serene setting of oaks and tropical plants nestling in the center of New Iberia, the town that sprouted on Town Farm plantation. Eight magnificent columns appear to be in full command of its west facade which faces the street that was once the Old Spanish Trail used by travelers migrating west from Florida. The rear of the mansion (its east side) faces the peaceful and picturesque Bayou Teche and surrounding the house on all sides are tranquil gardens that could give good reason to appropriately entitle the entire picture, "Techeland's Tranquil Eden."

PLANTATION BLACKSMITH

ROSEDOWN

Rosedown

The lush perfumed woodlands of the Felicianas embellished with an abundance of wild birds and flowers became a garden of paradise for painter-naturalist John James Audubon. And, just as the land brought a wealth of inspiration to Audubon, the Felicianas brought great monetary riches to cotton planters of the area. With those fortunes they were able to build elaborate mansions and beautiful gardens, some of them were considered to be among the most outstanding country houses in America...."*Rosedown*" is one of those marvelous plantation homes.

The wedding of Daniel and Martha Turnbull on November 13, 1828 united two of the pioneer families of West Feliciana Parish. Martha was the granddaughter of Olivia Ruffin barrow, a wealthy widow of Halifax County, North Carolina, who had brought her family to the Felicianas in 1797, taking with her a wealth of gold, prized household possessions and dozens of slaves in a private caravan of thirty covered wagons. Her children became prominent leaders of plantation life as early as 1801. One of Olivia's sons was William Barrow III who owned Locust Grove and Highland plantations; this was Martha Turnbull's father. Her mother was Pheraby Hilliard, daughter of a wealthy planter of Northampton County, North Carolina.

Daniel Turnbull was a highly educated son of John Turnbull, a native of Dumfrieshire, Scotland who became a successful planter on land obtained in the Felicianas by a Spanish grant.

While planning their home, Daniel and Martha chose W. Wright as their contractor and work began on November 1, 1834. They were careful to shop thoroughly and to choose the best of materials and furnishings. The cypress and cedar which came from a swamp woodland on their property was carefully picked, seasoned and milled at the plantation sawmill. The eighteen columns used on galleries and verandas were moulded and fluted by skilled plantations craftsmen. Bricks and hardware were also made on the plantation.

Elegant wall coverings and rugs were ordered from Paris, chandeliers of silver and statuary of marble came from Italy and the furniture was styled and crafted by the finest cabinetmakers of America.

Martha, who was an outstanding amateur horticulturist, ordered many exotic plants for her new gardens from Japan; importing some of the very first camelias into this country. She layed out her gardens in the patterns of those of French, Italian and English and statuary for the gardens were shipped in from Italy.

On May 1, 1835 their home was completed and it wasn't long before Martha's gardens also began to flourish. The total cost of the mansion amounted to $13,109.10. Inspired by a romantic play the couple had seen while honeymooning in Europe, they named their new home "Rosedown."

Daniel made a fortune on cotton, besides Rosedown he and Martha owned three other plantations; Inheritance, DeSoto and Styopa. The last two were located on Turnbull Island in the extreme northwest tip of West Feliciana Parish across the Mississippi River. Rosedown became the management center for his empire. It was the center for all business operations as well as for all social activities. There were elaborate dinners, elegant formal balls, informal parties, card games, women socials and musical concerts.

Other entertainments of the era included horse racing, hunting events with horses and dogs, horseback riding, carriage drives about the countryside and fishing trips. But, the most elaborately planned entertainments were the formal balls held in the spring and fall of each year when professional musicians were brought in by riverboat from New Orleans. These events were carefully planned for weeks, all under the direct supervision of the mistress of Rosedown, Martha Turnbull. They were the most popular events of the year and everyone of any social position for many miles around attended those gala affairs.

The Turnbulls had two children, a son and a daughter. Sarah, who was as beautiful as her mother, married James Bowman, son of William and Eliza Bowman of Oakley plantation. The son, William Turnbull, married Carolina Butler whose mother was great-granddaughter of Martha Washington. William became manager of the plantations on Turnbull Island. On November 12, 1856, while crossing Old River at DeSoto planation, William's skiff overturned and he was drowned.

Rosedown, a very productive plantation, was oriented around the money crop of the Felicianas, cotton. Work on the plantation required a rigid dependable routine. To grow cotton anywhere a planter had to depend on no less than one hundred twenty-two frost-free days. In West Feliciana, Daniel could count on as much as two hundred sixty frostless days. He owned an average of four hundred fifty slaves for his operations. He maintained a gin on Rosedown. After the seed was removed the cotton was pressed into four hundred pound bales which was shipped to the Manchester mills of England via New Orleans and Liverpool. From Rosedown alone he averaged from four hundred to four hundred twenty-five bales each year.

To help ease the ever present problems of maintaining good health among his slaves, Daniel Turnbull built a doctor's office and hired a physician to care for the ills of some five hundred people.

Slave cabins were well built and laid out in a plan of a small city. His slaves were well cared for as Daniel Turnbull believed in good health and comfort for his workers. He built them a church and a community center for their frolicking. But, some of the slaves did attend church services at Grace Episcopal Church in St. Francisville. A baptist minister was also engaged to hold regular Sunday morning services for them at their church on Rosedown.

The very successful planter, husband and father Daniel Turnbull died on October 30, 1861, leaving his wife with much wealth. And, she was also left to face alone the oncoming woes, social attacks and economic upheavals brought on by the Civil War. Martha was to live another thirty-five years bearing those hardships, sorrows, traumas and deteriorating conditions of her beloved Rosedown and to watch the flowers fade away in her beautiful European gardens.

For the next sixty years, against staggering odds, the beautiful old mansion and gardens were to survive only because of the strong wills, hardwork and prayers of the heirs, four unmarried daughters of Sarah Turnbull Bowman; Carrie, Isabel, Sarah and Nina. Nina, the last of those daughters, died at the age of eighty-seven on June 30, 1955. In spite of all the hardships that were encountered during those long years and against tremendous odds, at Nina's death there was not one single mortgage or bill left outstanding. This was a very grand tribute paid by four honorable sisters to the memory and dignity of their noble ancestors.

The late Catherine Fondren Underwood purchased Rosedown mansion and gardens in the spring of 1956. She was a godsend, not only for the survival of Rosedown, but to reincarnate this historic treasure and gardens to the original state of splendor and beauty that had once surrounded this grand mansion of St. Francisville in the Felicianas.

PIGEONNAIRE

The Amazing Valcour Aime

The title "Prince of Louisiana Planters" was not one that was carelessly awarded, it was a title that was well earned by a noble Louisiana Frenchman by the name of Valcour Aime. His generous contributions to Louisiana agriculture and to the sugar cane industry were outstanding and the day-by-day diary which he kept became the "Planter's Bible" for many decades after his death. It was a hallmark to his successes as a sugar cane planter.

His christening name was "Gabriel" but this was changed to Valcour at a very early age by a mulattress nurse at his father's plantation and he carried that name with him to his grave. No one ever knew where she got it or what it meant, but his name became the most honored in Louisiana's plantation land during the 1800's. Perhaps if Noah Webster would have assessed Valcour's life and accomplishments he would have written his name into the dictionary and defined it, "a man of regal character with distinguished wisdoms and many noble achievements."

Valcour's father was François Aime, a native of France who had settled on the west bank of the Mississippi in St. James Parish. His mother, Marie Julia Fortier was the daughter of Michel Fortier II, also a French immigrant. In 1798 a son was born to the young couple....that son was to become that prince of Louisiana agricultural society.

At the age of three Valcour's father died and his mother took him to live with Grandpère Fortier in New Orleans. His grandfather raised him until he was nineteen years of age and during that time Valcour received the finest in education, and he learned well. Not only did he speak excellent Parisian French but he also learned the English language in absolute fashion. He was a brilliant student in all aspects of his training.

Before he reached twenty years of age he had returned to his father's plantation to take over operations. His father's holdings had been bequeathed to him and he was eager to take command. Among his neighbors was the Roman family, one of the young girls was named Joséphine, sister of Jacques Telesphore Roman, builder of Oak Alley and André Bienvenue Roman who became Governor of Louisiana. Valcour set his sights on this petit and pretty Creole girl and before long he had wooed Joséphine into matrimony. In spite of height difference (he was six feet three inches tall and she was five feet two inches) they fell deeply in love and from the very first day that marriage was a success.

Joséphine adapted to her role very quickly, proudly and ably she became the mansion's mistress who ruled the plantation manor and supporting facilities with a smooth, firm hand. This allowed Valcour to fully concentrate his talents on the productivity of fields and mills. She honored her husband with four pretty daughters in succession, and then a son. Their names; Edvige, Joséphine, Emma, Felicité and the son, Gabriel. All received excellent educations from private tutors, with higher learnings from St. Michaels Convent for the girls and Jefferson College for "Gabi," as he was called by family and friends. Gabi also received further schooling in Paris.

Valcour and Joséphine named their plantation "Petite Versailles" and called the sugar mill St. James Refinery. On the plantation in 1853 there were two hundred fifteen slaves; 107 field and mill workers, 2 coopers, 2 blacksmiths, 2 engineers, 4 carpenters, 20 house and garden servants, 4 nurses, 11 elderly men and women who attended the stables, poultry yards, commissary and cared for the small children. There were also 64 children under the age of five years.

Because of their ability to better learn the technical aspects of operations, several white workers were entrusted to the complicated apparatus and machinery of the mills, these were German and Acadian men.

Sugar, the main crop, was a year round operation on the plantation, but by no means was it the only product for marketing. Aime also produced large quantities of corn, oats, cotton, hay and vegetables. Cattle and sheep were also raised for market and for the plantation needs. Valcour built a large sugarhouse made of brick to process his sugar and a sawmill to produce lumber for construction. The plantation had a total of fifteen thousand arpents of land (an arpent is a French measurement that is slightly less than a U.S. acre). Petite Versailes was a very self-sustaining plantation of unusual output and by the time he was thirty years of age Valcour had become one of the most successful and influential planters in the South. Before reaching the age of fifty he had been honored with the title "Prince of Planters," a title not easily accepted by this gracious and humble man.

He pioneered the plantation railway system; in 1833, when the entire world had less than one thousand miles of railroad, the Aime plantation had an entire railroad system to serve the refinery. There was also a private railroad passenger service from the riverboat landing to his mansion for receiving business people and friends. The Aime family riverboat transported friends and relatives to and from New Orleans.

A considerable portion of his land was left to a wilderness of virgin timber and swamp, disturbing this only for purposes of hunting, and, when absolutely necessary, the removal of cypress trees, to make lumber for buildings and other wood products. The task of manufacturing was great and included the making of hogsheads (barrels for sugar and syrup), shingles for roofing, fence pickets and rails, and the making of bricks was a routine operation. Over a million pounds of refined sugar was produced at the mill each year. According to records of his diary in 1853 alone the sugarhouse produced one million, eight hundred and sixty-seven thousand pounds of refined sugar. This grossed approximately $100,000.00 in sugar alone. Thousands of bushels of corn, beans and other produce were shipped to world markets each years. To exemplify the extremely high efficiency of the Aime plantation; equal acreage and productivity of other plantations would have required nearly twice the number of slaves.

A pioneer in the development of refined sugar he used steam equipment to the fullest at his mills. He developed a method for making highly refined sugar from watermelon juice which was very successful, but in his own words "this was not very practical due to the low yield per acre." He developed new and more effective cultivating and irrigating methods with elaborate flooding systems using water from the Mississippi River. It was one of the most opulent, successful and self-sustaining plantations of the 1800's.

Valcour was an extremely successful self-made horticulturist who experimented extensively with numerous varieties of plants. His hothouses were exceptional and always thriving with new species. He was an extraordinary practical chemist and an expert in the science of agriculture. Being of such unusual intelligence and ability, his friends and neighbors felt they lived in the shadow of a monarch. It was very difficult for them to compete with his brilliance and his genius.

The "big house," Madame Aime's domain, was an excellent example of a Creole household of upper class culture. The family and its comforts were most important, their needs came first. But the Aime's were excellent hosts to all visitors, friends and business people alike, all guests were made to feel important. Each morning they were awakened with a steaming cup of Creole coffee, and always on each tray was a fresh red rose from the gardens. At each dining plate there was a large fresh flower, preferably a camelia for the ladies. One visitor, authoress Eliza Ripley, wrote of the plantation, *"I was never made to feel more important, I want to remember the Valcour Aime home and its charming hospitality as I saw it and loved it.... when I waved my last adieu."*

The two and one-half story home was elaborately furnished with the finest of statuary, silver and crystal chandeliers, marble mantels, gold frame mirrors, mahogany and marble stairways and richly carved furniture of mahogany, cedar and cherry. The house had sixteen rooms and a large ballroom floored with marble. The lower gallery was tiled with black and white marble diamonds. Secret stairways were built into thick walls. Courtyards were shaded and wide spacious galleries were supported by large round columns.

Magnificent gardens and orchards displayed an astonishing array of plants and animal life. There were rippling streams, rambling walkways, arched bridges, decorated pagodas, marble statues and flowers bloomed everywhere. Oriental vines embraced great trees and climbed high into the oaks while Spanish moss dripped from massive limbs. Tall palms waved gracefully to the passersby on the river. Hundreds of rose bushes shrouded with flowers flavored the air with rich perfumes.

Black and white swans glided elegantly across peaceful lagoons. Peacocks adorned the landscape with colorful feathery fans and hundreds of egrets and herons feasted on crawfish and minnows in nearby man-made terrapin ponds. Deer, rabbits, ostriches and kangaroos (shipped from Africa and Australia) played together in heavily fenced pastures. Tropical birds of various species fluttered about in specially constructed aviaries. Off in an secluded corner of the plantation was a vast sanctuary of wild birds and animals; ducks, geese, snipe and other game birds from the north flocked to this refuge during the winter months.

Fruit and nuts were in abundance; pecans, walnuts, mangoes, pineapples, plums, oranges, peaches, figs, bananas and others. Coffee and tobacco plants enriched the zestful desires of the Creole habits. Besides the many species of flowering shrubs and exotic plants, the Aime gardens boasted the very first camphor trees of North America, shipped to them from Korea.

Delicious cheeses and other dairy foods were plentiful and on the dining tables were fine wines and brandies made from the fruit of private vineyards and orchards. Delicious cakes and candies of all kinds were products of their kitchens. The forerunner to the famed "praline" was the very popular "sweet" at plantation sugarhouse parties. The young people delighted in stringing shelled pecans together then dipping these strings into boiling syrup vats.... after cooling, these were savored as delicious candy coated nuts. "Cuite," a thick cane syrup, almost to the point of crystalization, was used for making a favorite taffy candy.

Family entertainments were lavish and plentiful; formal balls, informal parties, sugarhouse "soirées" at grinding time, lawn parties, horseback riding, carriage tours along the river and ice skating parties on the frozen batture during the freezing days of wintertime. The private riverboat "Gabi" made frequent journeys to and from New Orleans with visiting guests. Members of the Aime family attended the theatre, opera and concerts in New Orleans and shopped at the city's finest department stores and boutiques.

Valcour Aime was a compassionate and just man who treated his slaves with deep favor and concern for their health and welfare. They were well fed and well clothed and when work on the plantation slackened they were given extra time off for personal chores and duties. He was a charitable man who gave much of his love and of his wealth to those in need. He set aside many days throughout the year to spend with his slaves; New Year's Day being one of his favorite times with them because it was on that day he would give to them special gifts for the Yuletide Season. It would raise his spirits to see them happy.

On work days the slaves on Petite Versailles were allowed a half hour for breakfast and two hours for dinner (lunch) and were served from the field kitchens. There were alloted acreages for community crops and time off to work and harvest those crops. In 1837 the total harvest of Aime corn was 4,200 barrels while the harvest of slave corn was 2,300 barrels and 100 carts of pumpkins. In 1841 the slave crop yielded 3,000 barrels of corn. They were allowed to keep all profits derived from those crops and in addition were allowed to have vegetable gardens, poultry and pigs for private use. (One slave raised a hog that weighed over 700 pounds). Aime furnished them all necessary housing, clothing, food and medical care. The slave hospital had broad galleries, wards and private rooms for those who were gravely ill. There were four full time trained nurses and a doctor from New Orleans made regular visits by the riverboat "Gabi" for routine and emergency medical care.

In 1830 Valcour Aime helped to establish the "College of Jefferson," he was on the board of directors and was one of five who drafted its first constitution. In 1859, when the college was beginning to fail financially, he purchased the land and its facilities and then donated it to the state which by special Louisiana Legislature took over financial operational responsibilities of the college. During the Civil War it was confiscated and occupied by Federal troops. Again, in 1864, Valcour obtained the college and immediately donated it to the Marist Fathers, a Roman Catholic organization which established it as St. Mary's Jefferson College, a religious institution for higher education of sons of Louisiana planters. It was in 1859 that Valcour had the little Gothic chapel built on the campus to honor his deceased children.

It was because of this donation to education and because of his stubborn persistence toward the survival of this college that this magnificently beautiful edifice still exists as a religious institution. Without a doubt, today it would not be even a memory had it not been for his determined efforts and generous donations. His contributions to education and to religious establishments were not limited to Jefferson College. There were many more generous donations of food and finances to St. Michaels Convent where his daughters attended. St. James Roman Catholic Church on the west bank of the river became the most richly furnished in Louisiana. He imported altar ornaments, tall gold candelabras and fine Italian paintings of the Stations of the Cross for the church. His gardens endlessly furnished an abundance of sweet scented blooms for flowering bouquets for the church vases on rich marble pedestals. And he also made many generous financial contributions of perpetual nature.

When each of the Aime daughters got married they received a plantation and home as a wedding gift from their parents. Every year at Christmas time each one of them would find beneath their plate a generous amount of money. Gabi only lived to his early twenties, he died of yellow fever in 1853 and within two years his mother, Joséphine, and his sisters Felicité and Edvige followed in death. Complete collapse of mind and spirit came to Valcour, his ambitions and enthusiasms died with them. His feverish hunger to accomplish vanished and the happy nature of Monsieur Aime ceased to exist. Although he lived another sixteen years his productive spirits went with his dear ones to their graves.

Valcour Aime loved to attend Mass; his favorite service being on Christmas Eve, which he never missed. Midnight Mass on Christmas of 1866 was no exception and although the weather was icy cold he journeyed through drizzling rain to the little church he had embellished so generously with furnishings and donations to fulfill his Yuletide duties. This gaunt figure took his place unnoticed at the rear of the church unmindful of the grim coldness of his wet clothing.... he had become bathed in the warmth of his granddaughter Christine's golden voice which rose delightfully rich above all in the choir that sang praises to the newborn King. Valcour was deeply pleased. When mass ended he walked slowly to the little nearby cemetery and in soaked clothing he kneeled gently before the graves of his beloved wife and children, as he had done so many times before. This would be the last Christmas visit he would make.

The eminent Valcour Aime died of pneumonia on New Year's Day of 1867, one day of the year he had always favored.... he was sixty-eight years of age. His death signalled the passing of one of the most revered, loved and most influential of all Louisiana planters.

His plantation diary became a very valuable instrument to society, not just for the culture and processing of sugar cane and other farm products, but for its calendar of preventative measures; daily temperatures, droughts, freezes and rainfall records served as a guide to long range predictions and estimates of conditions for future planting seasons and crop culture.

His contributions to the agricultural industry, to religion, to education, to the dignity and culture of the state and to the development of Louisiana are unmeasureable.... but they were never ever justly honored. Existing today are memorials that are not properly displayed or hearlded; a road marker at the site where his home and gardens were once located, now overgrown by a wild jungle, is barely noticeable to the passerby; his family tomb in the little cemetery across the road from the present church is very sadly neglected, and there is no credit or tribute displayed to publicly honor him as benefactor of Jefferson College (now Manresa Retreat) on the east bank of the Mississippi River near Convent, Louisiana.

For such a magnitude of accomplishments and contributions by a man who gave so much of himself for the sake of his fellow man and for future generations, it seems so very sad and shameful that his memory could not be honored in a better fashion of gratitude. This lack of acknowledgment certainly does not reflect dignified behaviors of an intelligent, civilized and appreciative Christian society. His distinguished services to mankind surely merits a far more honorable position in Louisiana's history pages.

* * * * * * * *

"They came to eagerly partake of his love, his kindness, his labors, his generosity and of the gifts of wisdom that God had bestowed upon him. When his heart became sad and broken, his spirits low, and when his health had succumbed to nature's devastating elements they cast aside the memory of his name and walked away with the fruits of his genius."

A BLEND OF OLD NEW ORLEANS FLAVORS

Visit Old New Orleans

[NOTE: This composition is designed to take the reader on a present day visit into the Vieux Carre, which is the original old New Orleans. Most of the districts and buildings still exist as they were then, giving the reader a realistic journey into the early years of this antique French town.]

Come back with me into time to visit old New Orleans during the 1800's and you will see a unique place set aside in this nation for man to behold with an obsession of selfish claim. You will see a place so far removed from any other on this earth, and you will be stricken in awe at its queer state of existence. She is the Queen of the great Mississippi and you shall become one of her most obedient subjects.

Approaching the old French town from the river we cannot see her "coast" because of the multitudes of sails, masts, smokestacks and makeshift houses on barges. There are boats and ships of every kind, from pirogues to the tall ones, from flatboats to sternwheelers loaded with hundreds of bales of cotton on the decks.

Edging its way through this conglomerate of vessels our boat slips into a berth at the foot of St. Peter Street. It is as though the Port Master knew we were coming and had reserved this spot especially for us, it is the only empty berth in sight.

On the docks are countless tons of cargoes of every kind. Some are for local merchant shops, others will travel to distant ports and foreign lands. There are thousands of cotton bales with as many barrels of sugar and molasses amid furs, lumber, kegs of rum and tobacco compressed into huge bundles. There are crates with bolts and bolts of fine silks, pongees, linens and woolens. Fruits of every kind lie among barrels and barrels of flour, as far as the eye can see. And there are hundreds of cases of fine wines, champagnes and brandies from France that will soon whet the appetites in stylish restaurants and at Creole tables of Louisiana.

There are sailors from afar and negro roustabouts from home, the rich man, the poor man, indians, brash laborers and a mixture of the refined with the crude; like the elegant looking lady with her planter husband in contrast to the lowly harlot luring a seaman into her crib.

We pause ashore and in disbelief we observe the mass of humanity and the magnitude of cargoes to be shipped. While meandering through to reach Decatur Street we dodge drays and wagons of every sort, staying alert for the speeding hack for hire. Over to the right is Place d'Armes where soldiers once paraded in full dress and in precision on these grounds laid out in 1722. Now it is a peaceful park with walkways, trees, flowers and a massive statue of the "Battle of New Orleans" hero astride a huge stallion. This tranquil park is Jackson Square bordered on three sides by noteworthy buildings. Here on St. Peter and on the far St. Ann Street we note the twin Pontalba buildings erected in 1849 by the Baroness Pontalba, the industrious and spirited daughter of Don Andres Almonaster y Roxas, nobleman of Andalusia of Spain, and the colony's richest man during the Spanish period. The two red brick structures are said to be the very first apartment buildings in the United States and are still being used for that purpose.

Across Jackson Square is that grand St. Louis Cathedral flanked by the Presbytère on its left and the Cabildo on its right. Both were used as the seat of government during the Spanish regime (1765-1801). The Presbytere was originally built for a monastary for Capuchin priests, but was never used for that purpose.

The church, erected in 1794, is the oldest cathedral in the United States. The passageway on the near side of the cathedral is appropriately named Pirates Alley. It was through this little alleyway that the many pirates of the river and of the Gulf made their way in darkness with contraband to be sold at reduced rates to waiting New Orleans' merchants. St. Antoine Alley on the far side of the church is so named honoring Père Antoine, one of New Orleans most beloved priests who died in 1829 at the age of eighty-one.

Turning on Chartres toward Canal Street we begin our walking journey of sights and excitements through this city of unusual cultures and unique structures and numerous legends. But, before we go too far we must see La Petite Theatre just across Chartres at 616 St. Peter Street. Its patrons proudly brag that it is the oldest continous little theatre group in the country.

Moving along, there are the numerous cafes and coffee houses (saloons) where merchants, farmers, pirates and travelers idle their time away. 538 Chartres is the very spot where the great fire of 1788 began with a simple flame from a religious house altar and quickly spread to encompass and destroy eight hundred fifty-six buildings in French Town, New Orleans.

On the corner at St. Louis, 500 Chartres, is a house that was built specifically for Napoleon Bonaparte who was to exile himself from his troubled France. It was never used for that purpose since the ill Napoleon died on the Island of St. Helena before his journey to New Orleans.

Just across St. Louis Street at the corner on Chartres is the famed Masperos Exchange, (1788). This is one of the most popular coffee houses of the city and was frequently visited by such celebrated figures as Andrew Jackson and pirates Jean and Pierre Laffite. From the kitchens of Masperos the famed *Louisiana gumbo* was first concocted and the *pousse café* was invented. In this original exchange stood one of the country's most celebrated auction blocks with sales of goods made in three different languages; French, Spanish and English. Many elegant prizes of contraband was auctioned at the Maspero Exchange with prominent figures attending.

The streets of the Vieux Carré are litterly covered with a sea of humanity. There are Frenchmen and Spaniards, West Indians and Creoles. There are lawyers, clergymen, priests, friars and nuns. There are negroes in fine clothing and there are river rats in rags mingling among the multitudes of pirates, assassins, gamblers, drunkards, sailors and robbers. There are pretty girls from the fine Creole homes and there are those from lavish or gaudy bordellos. There are the wealthy and there is the beggar, all making up this unusual ocean of mankind collected from every nation in the world.

That grand building seen on St. Louis between Chartres and Royal is the St. Louis Hotel. It matches the fame and elegance of the St. Charles Hotel of the American sector. It was built in 1835, gutted by fire in 1841 and rebuilt again into greater splendor to become the social and political center of the South and in the year 1874 it became the State Capitol. The capitol was moved to Baton Rouge in 1882 and the building will in the future be renovated and renamed Hotal Royale.

Crossing over Chartres at Conti, walking toward Royal we come upon a vision of the past, and it is so hard to believe that it does not become a reality all over again. We can clearly hear the singing of steel rapiers upon one another in duels as they did so regularly just a few decades ago. This is Exchange Alley where many schools of fencing exist in this passageway that extends from St. Louis to Iberville. These are schools for the Creoles who so courageously defend their French culture at the drop of a glove or because of a naughty glance at one of their Creole Belles. Here are the academies of such greats in fencing as Pèpe Lulla, Marcel Dauphin, Titol, Bastile Croquere, the incomparable Gilbert Rosiere and many others. Those who so capably taught the young and old alike in the art of defense by dueling with sword or the pistol.

Walk down Exchange Alley with its history of academies, saloons, cafes and onto Exchange Place, between Custom House and Canal streets, where there are as many business transactions as any other place in America. Crops, stocks and merchandise change into more hands here than any other place. This is millionaire's alley, the financial district of Old French Town.

Walk up Iberville and onto Royal to visit the many shops of fine apparel on both sides of the street amid many luxurious restaurants. The dwellings above the shops are exquisite, exhibiting lace design ironwork and railings with balconies adorned with massive urns of fern and tropical plants. Alleyways between the shops lead to elegant patios of greenery, as we have seen at 617 Chartres. Up the way on Royal at number 520 we see another of these courtyards encircled by tropical greenery with gaily painted shuddered windows and arched doors.

These streets of the French Quarter are essentially just as they were when first laid out by Adrien DePauger in 1724. Only small insignificant changes have been made since, but they have been elaborately dressed with interesting people and superb dwellings. The streets measure thirty-eight feet in width and have been paved with granite stones shipped from Belgium, now covering those once muddy paths. The "banquettes" of boardwalks fronting the shops have been replaced with flagstone and motar throughout the Old Town making it very pleasant wherever one may walk.

Across Royal at number 127 is the birthplace of the Krewe of Comus, the oldest carnival organization in the city, founded in 1857. It is the Krewe of Comus that first organized the famed street parades of the carnival season on January 10, 1857. Little more need to be said here about Mardi Gras, its history is covered further on in this chapter under the title, "Mardi Gras - 'Fat Tuesday."

This city is known throughout the world for its superb foods and many fine restaurants. One is housed in a building at 417 Rue Royal, and another is up the way, 713 St. Louis between Royal and Bourbon. The latter is the world reknown "Antoines," founded by the Alciator family in 1840.

Let us rest for a while before we continue our tour through these old streets. Perhaps you'd care for a Sazerac or a Gin Fizz created here in New Orleans, or one of the many other refreshing drinks of this quaint Old Town. Maybe a Cafe au Lait or Café Brûlot or a Biere Douce. Or should we take the time for one of the fine meals of Courbouillon, Boullabaisse or a great dish of rice and okra with the finest sauces you'll ever find? The seafood and pastries are the best in the world so do not hesitate even though the menus are printed in French, whatever you choose will delight your taste buds.

To meander into the rear of these fine eating or drinking places you will often find games of chance and gambling skills. There may even be those fashionable professionals who travel the river on the steamboats; such famous names as Jimmy Fitzgerald (known as the best dressed riverboat gambler on the Mississippi), Gib Cohern, John McClane, Tom Mackey and many others, with their polished mannerisms who come to challenge the many Creoles who greatly indulge in the games of chance. Ship's cargoes, large salaries and many fine plantations have been won and lost over and over again in these streets lined with shops and coffee houses. The Creoles of New Orleans and of Lòuisiana greatly love to pass their time and money over the many tables of chance.

Along Royal there are many more elegant shops with fine living quarters above. All over Old French Town below the balconies on supporting posts can been seen needle sharp metal spurs that have been welded along the posts. These were put there to discourage the many pirates and vagrants who frequently climb to the balconies above in efforts to assault the fine ladies of the Creole merchants. Look for those spurs, most have been removed, but some can still be seen high on the posts. Perhaps this did discourage some of the offenders, but many were graciously obliged by accommodating females of "dignified" Creole culture who lowered ropes of bed sheeting tied together for their "visitors" convenience. Unsuspecting husbands below in their shops were unaware of the daring ventures of their ladies who were "safely" housed above them in undisturbed peace, protecting their "chaste" morals.

Number 529 Royal is the Casa Miro House built in 1784 for Governor Esteban Miro who served Louisiana from 1785 to 1791. At the rear of the cathedral and on Royal is the Garden of St. Anthony. Here, many a rival duelist lost his life to a victor who had won a quadroon mistress, or, one who had lost the argument over properties and values of his family heritage. Duels were fought here for just about any reason that challenged honor, no excuse was too frail.

Turning down Toulouse we walk to Bourbon Street to see the French Opera House standing in all its glory. Its doors were opened on December 1, 1859 with the presentation of "William Tell." Since that time it has become the center of social life, not only in New Orleans, but also for the entire South. It has for a long time been the scene of many fabulous carnival balls. (Sadness will come upon America when this great structure of culture will burn to the ground in 1919).

At number 717 Orleans is that famed Quadroon Ballroom in the Theatre d'Orleans (1818). Here at these Quadroon balls many mistresses were chosen by rich French merchants or planters who housed and supported them in neat one story Creole houses along Rampart and Burgundy between Orleans and Esplanade. A mulatto woman may have lived here an entire lifetime as a concubine, in respected dignity.

Returning to Royal on the corner of St. Ann we note with significant importance that in the year 1800, in a candy shop on this corner, the candy made with Creole pecans known worldwide as *New Orleans' praulines* were first sold. And too, at this corner stood the famous Café des Exiles that specifically patronized all exiles from foreign lands regardless of their race, creed or color.

Wandering through these streets with old and beautiful buildings we often see in the rear other interesting structures that seem to surround the courtyards and patios. Some are quarters used by house servants, or may be a kitchen to the main house or again it could be the equivalent to the plantation garconnaire; the latter being additional quarters for young men of the family to entertain in privacy and to exploit their manhood with young mulatto servant girls or Creole Belles with loose values. Passages from the streets to the courtyards are carriage ways to the stables in the rear of the complex.

At Dumaine we turn off Royal to the right and visit number 632, a French colonial residence (1726) which has been given the notable name of "Madame John's Legacy." This home is the oldest building in the Mississippi Valley and is typical of early construction in the suburbs and on Colonial Louisiana plantations.

902-910 Rue Royal is the Heine House (1838) where a princess was born. Born and growing up in this home was the later-to-become Princess of Monoco, Alice Heine of Louisiana heritage.

Continue on Royal to St. Philip and turn up one block to Bourbon, to see the blacksmith shop used by Jean and Pierre Laffite as a cover for their black market business operations. Dealings that took them to distant Louisiana bayous and plantations to deliver smuggled goods from other lands. Their shops where contraband goods were for sale in New Orleans can be seen in the five and six hundred blocks of Royal, and too, in Chartres Street there is another. We have passed them on our way.

Back to Royal we meander cautiously over to number 1140 (1835) which has so appropriately been named "Haunted House." Here lived the infamous Madam LaLaurie who was so sadistically depraved, cruelly persecuting her slaves in chains and whipping them unmericfully day and night into unconsciousness. When they would regain their senses she would nurse and feed them back to health only to again whip them without mercy, shrieking in hilarious ecstasy at the presence of their pain. For these inhuman endeavors she was driven in madness from New Orleans by Creoles who sought to lynch her, but she escaped to France and was later killed in a wild boar hunt. But those treacherous nights of implacable pleasures still haunt the Old French Town and if you listen carefully you can still hear in the night the many moans and painful screams of the slaves amid loud cracks of a rawhide whip and the sadistic cries of fiendish laughter that accompany them.

Move away from this scene of inhuman cruelty and meander on to the corner of Barracks and Decatur streets to see the rear of the U. S. Mint. It has operated from 1838 until 1862, then once again from 1879 and will not close its doors until 1910. At its peak it produced $5,000,000 in coin per month.

Between Barracks Street and Ursulines a half block to the river from Decatur we are upon Gallatin Street. I must take some time to try to tell you of this place of undescribable state of degeneracy. We dare not enter and will remain at some distance where our safety is assured.

Here lies the cesspool of our state, where every member of corrupt morals collect in the gutters, streets, saloons, flop houses, dance halls and cheap boarding houses. This is where the sewer rats cannot be distinguished from the human element that carries as much and more disease and certainly is far more detrimental to humanity.

Cubicles are built with cargo boxes where whores carry on a routine business day and night. This wicked sewer harbors ruffians from flatboats, lowly sailors from far out vessels and criminals of all sorts crawl everywhere while painted harlots slither over cheap dance hall floors in short calico dresses with nothing underneath. They will drug or murder a person for the few pennies in his pockets. They make their own laws and execute those who defy their exploits. For sixty cents, a man can get a drink, a woman and a bed for the night and if he has any more money left he usually finds himself on the following morning lying in the gutter naked and penniless.....if he is lucky.

It is a festering sore with cesspools of criminals crawling like maggots in the night through the hallways, gutter, dance halls and gin mills, forever looking for a careless victim to pounce on and devour. So let us move away quickly, not far from here exists an atmosphere far more pleasant; a complete contrast to this grim disgusting and shameful scene that lasted until 1890.

At the corner of Ursuline and St. Philip we see that stately, dignified and famous convent of the Ursulines. It is so well known for its many fine products of womanhood. It has become the structure of cultural upbringing for many fine young girls who have become mothers of many great Creole families. It is known as the birthplace of Louisiana culture. This old convent was built in 1734 for the Ursuline nuns for a school of higher training for young girls, many of whom were orphans of early Louisiana. It is the first Catholic school for young girls in the United States. Ah-h, it is so well preserved as a shrine to those elegant ladies of tasteful culture and superb character!

St. Ann and Decatur (riverside) brings us to the French Market erected in 1822 especially for Choctaw Indians and German traders (from the German Coast upriver from New Orleans) to sell their furs, crafts, pottery and food products to the residents and visitors of New Orleans. It has since been occupied by Italian and Sicilian vegetable-fish vendors.

Having walked so far along these streets perhaps we must rest a while or return to the riverboat. But, there is much time before it will be leaving the dock, returning home. There is more yet to see in this Old Town and we can do this while we rest. We will hire a carriage and it will be a pleasant ride!

We take one near the French Market and travel up St. Ann Street where there are many more old homes that have such appeal and distinction. We see Creole cottages of unique design and some that are known as "shotgun" houses, one room wide and several rooms deep, one behind the other. This is a design for comfort and air circulation. A typical "double" shotgun can be seen at 818 Dumaine.

And, to our right on Burgundy we come upon the famed Quadroon single story domiciles, all painted so neatly in white, many have hanging pots with blooming plants and window curtains of flowered organdy. These are the dedicated mistresses who are "kept" by their white Creole "husbands." It is a pleasant and happy section with many beautiful women of almond colored skin walking about the streets with colorful dresses and shopping baskets. These are the ever so celebrated concubines we have heard about in whisper. There are many more of these little homes around the corner on Rampart and other streets in the direction of Esplanade.

Toward Rampart on St. Ann we approach a small Creole cottage of much fame that has been spoken of many many times in whispering tales. This is the cottage of Marie Laveau the most celebrated of all voodooiennes. She was voodoo's queen and it is rumored that many secret meetings have taken place behind these walls and in the rear yard. Meetings that would decide the fate of many or the fate of the few; and some of social and political prominence.

We will not cast doubt or suspicion and move on without delay or notice..... those whispering rumors that we've often heard may be true!

Across Rampart Street is Beauregard Square, not too long ago this was Congo Square. It was here that the Sunday afternoon air was filled with sounds of the Calinda and the Bamboula, where the negroes congregated to dance their voodoo rituals and sing their voodoo songs. These were festive occasions and hundreds of whites came to view these "innocent" and exciting celebrations. There were vendors who sold beer, pies, lemonades and other refreshments.

The most celebrated of all male voodoo dancers was Bras Coupé, a large and strong black man with great vitality, but none ever came to such heights in popularity as their queen, Marie Laveau.

We ride along Rampart until we reach St. Louis and turn to Basin Street just past the canal basin where boats come into the city through Carondelet Canal and Bayou St. John from Lake Ponchartrain. This is only one of the many waterways dug by hearty Irish immigrants who came to this fair city looking for work and remained to make their home in the "Irish Channel," (that little community near the river in the American section) becoming another important segment of this curious and unusual city created in swamplands. Here too is a collection of every element of humanity that is imaginable. There are many ruffians and sailors as can be expected at any port. But, we continue along Basin to that much publicized and wicked *STORYVILLE, U.S.A.*

This section bounded by Basin Street, North Robertson, the Carondelet Canal and Iberville Street will become the most celebrated red light district in America. Here will be the most elaborate bordellos and here will be the lowest of cribs. Within these bounds we will find the finest of homes furnished with velvets, crystals, carpets, drapes, mirrored walls and ceilings and expensive furniture ornamented with the prettiest and most able prostitutes ever to be found anywhere. And within these bounds will be the crummiest of houses and "cribs" furnished only with a bunk, wash basin and kerosene lamps, over-the-hill and disgustingly uncouth whores crawling everywhere. The best of houses in Basin Street and the lowest of cribs in North Robertson and St. Louis near the canal. Houses with prices ranging from fifty dollars a night for the finest in flesh to twenty-five cents for the filthiest of whores. There will be music of all types including the Razy Dazy Spasm Bands that will roam the streets with their make-shift instruments playing for the pennies thrown to them by the passerby.

Storyville will be a showplace of New Orleans at the beginning of the 1900's. A place perhaps to visit, perhaps to patronize, perhaps to whisper about in the future, but surely a place that will never be forgotten by those who had been there.

As we leave this area we note that on Basin Street between St. Louis and Conti there is a cemetery with its graves built in typical New Orleans fashion, above ground due to the high level of below surface water. This is St. Louis Cemetery Number One (1788), it has become widely known because of the number of celebrated personalities buried here. Domonique You the famous pirate, favorite of Jean Laffite - Etienne de Boré, local planter who first successfully granulated sugar - Chalmette, of Battle of New Orleans fame, and more recently the famous voodoo queen Marie Laveau.

Crossing over to North Rampart Street, there on the corner of Conti is a very celebrated little church, Our Lady of Guadeloupe (1826), especially built as a burial chapel for the St. Louis Cemetery we just visited. To bury the dead through St. Louis Cathedral was considered a health hazard to the parishoners and for that reason this burial church was constructed.

Returning to the river front we again pass many fascinating and interesting buildings and homes decorated with ironlace and latticed windows; many have curious stories about them and some have attaching tales that will never allow them to be the proud domicile they were meant to be. Such is one on the corner of Orleans at 716 Dauphine. It has been burdened for so very long with the haunting of that grotesque slaughter behind those walls of a Turkish nobleman and his beautiful harem girls. All were butchered one night with never a clue telling who had committed this bizarre murder. But until this very day, in the still of a sleeping night, if one listens carefully, there can be heard the sounds of the flageolet and finger cymbals amid the scents of incense and shrieking women voices in gay song and naked dance..... or can those shrills be sounds from the lips of beautiful Turkish girls in torturous death?

We must return to more pleasant atmospheres and sounds of enjoyment, such as the quiet and cozy café at Royal and Orleans where we shall leave our carriage and have a "pousse café" before we meander toward our waiting paddle-boat. We hate to leave, for it has been such an interesting and pleasant visit to this Old Town. But dusk is quickly falling upon us and soon the gas lights will be lit and time will be for the bells to ring out from the old cathedral tower and whistles will signal the departure of our vessel from the riverbanks that border this captivating town of Old New Orleans.

We must return soon, there is so much more to be seen. When we do, perhaps we can meander curiously into the faubourgs of the "foreigners,".... those Americans in their uptown *"Garden District."*

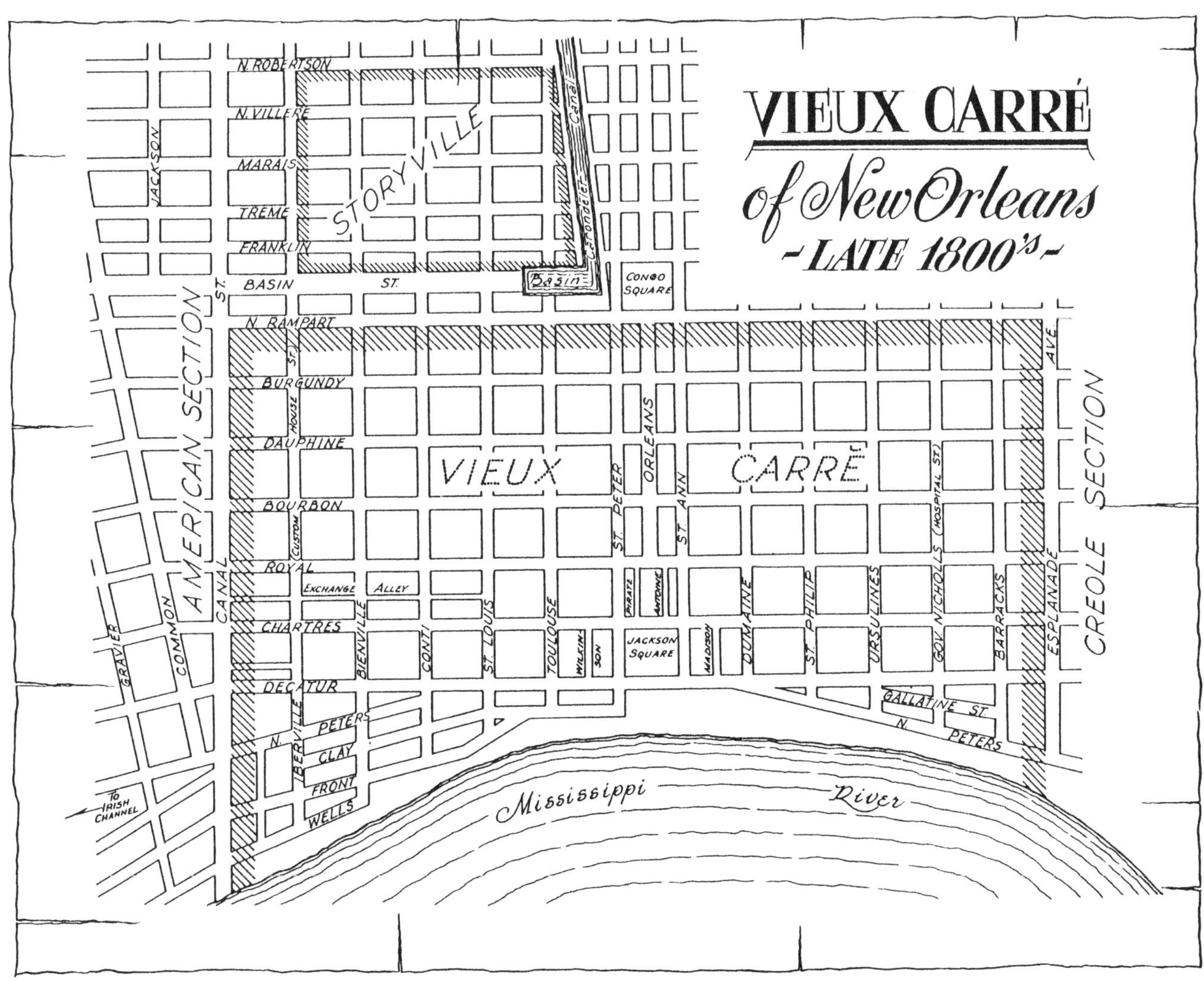

A "STORYVILLE" BORDELLO

Storyville, U.S.A.

The whining of clarinets, the drone of bass fiddles, the tinkling of piano keys and the brassy notes from trumpets and trombones, with an occasional intermingling of banjo strings. Screams of women in laughter of wicked gaiety and the wailing of female voices in songs of the blues.

These were the sounds in the nights of Storyville at the turn of the century.

Street whores, pimps and dope pushers, the laborer, the sailor, and the licentious scum; stylish "ladies of the evening," playboys, businessmen and sugar daddies all made up the scene of a district bounded by Basin Street, Iberville, North Robertson and St. Louis in New Orleans of the old. This was an area established to concentrate and control vice and crime.

Lavish bordellos decorated with fine furnishings of antiques, Persian rugs, oil paintings, sculptures and chandeliers of crystal. "Palaces" that housed elegant looking young girls adorned in revealing gowns of pongee, satin, silk and laces who vended their bodies for pleasures of the wealthy. Such mansions as Lulu White's *"Mahogany Hall,"* Josie Arlington's *"Grand Palace"* and Emma Johnson's *"Studio"* were among the delicately "refined" sporting houses for the rich.

In contrast to that "refinement" in prostitution there were the "crib girls," over-the-hill whores who operated from tiny decaying stalls furnished only with wash basin, oil lamp and cot. Doors and windows open, they revealed themselves in nakedness to all on the street, young and old alike, enticing them inside with suggestive gestures. There were tricks of teasing with the flesh and such mischievous pranks as snitching a hat from the passerby to lure him into their cribs. The price was cheap in coin but ever so costly in filth and disease.

A directory, the "Blue Book" by name, gave alphabetical listings of all "ladies" of Storyville houses, over seven hundred in all. White, octoroon, quadroon and negro women were named with addresses and their skills in sex.

The newspaper "Mascot" reported all happenings in the "district." It told of depraved orgies and sadistic "circus" acts performed to entertain guests. And it told of the madams, their ventures and their conflicts in efforts to rise to that pedestal of "Queen of the Whores."

"Vice and crime makes news and news makes vice and crime."

Storyville became the largest legal fleshpot of love and vice of any district in the country and it prospered well for nearly twenty years. It began in 1897 and was closed by federal order when America entered World War I in an effort to protect servicemen from the evils and diseases of the big city.

Storyville came to its end, but all that it harbored swelled like a festering sore into the dignity of the city. Street walkers in noble areas, prostitutes moved into neighborhoods of decent morals, call girls and bawds infested respectable hotel lobbies and railroad stations, madams became mistresses to the wealthy. Dope pushers, panderers and whores operated in alleyways and courtyards and this mass of corruption that had been imprisoned by the "district" spread throughout the city like wildfire. The world's oldest profession and its evils again became uncontrollable and efforts by the "do-gooders" with their cure-all solutions were once again fruitless.

"Closing the gates of a Storyville did not abolish prostitution and its vices. Through its back doors went this sinful element to operate unharnessed in respectable neighboring communities. Social ignorance and shames with associated corrupted morals prevail and contaminate the decent values of chaste minds."

New Orleans Jambalaya

From its ramparts the Vieux Carré has spread afar into the wetlands in all directions, beckoning to men from every nation, becoming a city that cares for them all; Indian, French, Spanish, German, Negro, Irish, American, Italian, Sicilian and others.

There have been many good fortunes and there have been times of depression and disaster. Tyrants have been suppressed, the wishful appeased and the faithful rewarded.

There are the swamps and the lakes, the bayous and marshes, with highlands (not very) and the very low lands. There's alligators, snakes, turtles, crawfish, herons, egrets and all kinds of other wildlife, human and otherwise.

There's oak trees of every kind all decorated with Spanish moss, magnolias with gigantic blooms and great cypresses with knobby little knees. There's lagoons with ducks and swans and there's pigeons, and pigeons and pigeons.....

The streets are covered with cobblestone and brick and then there's powdered shell and clay bordered by more restaurants, more coffee houses and more brothels than any other city in the country.

She has beautiful girls from France and Spain and the Quadroon mistress for the white planter. There are soft-skin Creole Belles who are born here and there are those who were raised on the bayous.

That limited number of "filles á la cassettes" (casket girls) were so prolifically fertile, while the Old Town's numerous strumpets were ever so sterile. Ha! Perhaps that is why the old city has claimed so many descendants of "angelic stock".....???

There's lots and lots of wood turnings and jigsaw trim; elaborate cornice work with hand carved doors, fireplace mantels well adorned and beautifully spiralled staircases. And, there are balconies one above the other dressed in cast-iron lace.

All about are curlicues, balustrades and banisters, with shutters (not blinds) over French doors and windows. There are dormers below belvederes and little picket fences in between. Bricks are placed between posts and mud behind weatherboards with tile and cypress roofs.

Sunbaked bricks are covered with plaster and, of course, there's "bousillage." The colonial of the Creoles have galleries and patios and the classic of the Americans have porches and courtyards.

There are stable gates and Porte Cochère and banquettes of wood planks or flagstone walkways. Grille work have monograms while iron posts have sharp little spurs, and standing alone are columns of doric nature.

The "shotgun single" could become a "double" or just as well as "camelback," and the servants house a garconnaire with a pretty mullatto mistress waiting inside.

There's Le Petite Theatre du Vieux Carré and there was the French Opera House with Antonio Rapetti, contrasting as much as the French Market with its German and Indian vendors.

There's Dixieland Jazz and the colorful Razy Dazy Spasm bands. There's bagnios or brothels with brightly painted harlots and, of course, there's lesbians and fairies together with pimps and madams. Saloons and cabarets have dancers, singers and circuses with all kinds of different clowns; those who try to be and those who don't have to.

Maskers cheer kings and queens at the balls while marching flambeaux bearers lead floats with krewes and floats with revelers and everybody wants to be someone else.

There's voodoos for the good and voodoos for the bad, there's gris-gris to get well and there's gris-gris to get sick, and there are queens with frogs, chickens and snakes while Calinda or Bamboula dancers wear seven pointed tignons.

There are Creoles who gamble a lot and there are Creoles who pray a lot...... then there's Creoles who pray a lot while they gamble a lot!

Cults have their places for orgies while religions have their churches of worship. Funerals are like nowhere else and graveyards are called *"Cities of the Dead."*

Milling together are actors, writers and poets; debutantes and dowagers; ladies of the evening and mistresses; planters, merchants and financiers; and an abundance of just plain folk.

There are gift shops and there are antique shops and there are vendors all over the street. There are artists and models of every kind; artists looking at models and models looking at artists, while visitors are watching them all.

Ships come in from every port to berth with all kinds of boats. There are pirogues, skiffs, flatboats, barges, tugboats and those with plenty of sails. There are big boats and there are tiny boats and the steamboats have big fat smokestacks.

There's poor boy sandwiches with that famous french bread; gumbo, seafood, red beans and rice and hundreds of delightful dishes; and there's Café au Lait and Pousse Café, Café Brûlot and Café du Chickory.... and don't forget Café du Monde.

Putting all these ingredients together while stirring real well can make up the greatest jambalaya of them all; concocted into that most delicious, spicy and tempting dish called, *"NEW ORLEANS."*

J DeHart

The Noble Po Boy

It was borne out from a need
to stretch a dish of food
Of leftover 'tatoes or beans
yet change the taste and mood.
First known as a Poor Boy sandwich
the impoverished did enjoy,
Then it took on richer fillings
that changed its name to Po Boy.

But, don't buy it ready made
'cause most likely you'll be fooled
By someone who knows so little
'bout fixing this splendid food.
Get youself the makings
and do not spare a thing,
Meats, spices and tasty likes
and sauces with a tang.

First you've got to know the bread
that's true and nobly French,
You've got to know its taste and shape
for such a regal san'ich.
It must be fat across the middle
and pointed at each end,
A golden soft and savory crust
that will hold a'lots within.

Get hams, cheeses or seafood meats
depends on what you like,
Mustards and peppers and onion rings
and spices of great delight.
Flavored pickles and crispy lettuce
perhaps you'll shred the leaves,
Zesty relish and green shallots
or others that's sure to please.

Now slice the full length of the loaf
a sharpened knife you'll use,
Open apart and remove some white
leave as little as you choose.
Careful not to break the nose
this you must retain,
You'll find it comes in handy
a'soppin' up remains.

Continued ....

Oh yes, before you do proceed
get yourself some wine,
Sherry, Sauterne or maybe Port
to sip from time to time.
Don't drink too much before you eat
you'll want to have it blend,
Those delicious meats and cheeses
from the beginning to the end.

Back to the bread you are
a vital part we know,
So size it up for what you'll need
with fillings that'll overflow.
And now is when the fun begins
and taste buds you do excite,
So have another sip of wine
to whet your appetite.

Spread some Creole mustard thick
lay down some hams and cheese,
Tomatoes, onion, catsup and pickles
and some crispy lettuce leaves.
Put on the other half of bread
and press to make compact,
Cut in half on a slant
and keep the two in tact.

Get plenty of paper napkins
before you begin to eat,
There'll be lots of juicy drippings
It's quite a tricky feat.
Now, pour yourself a glass of wine
and sit back and enjoy,
A meal that's fit for any king
that deliciously NOBLE PO BOY!

NUMBER NINE

PLANTATION LAWN PARTY

A Tribute To Jazz

Stately marble columns towering into the clouds, spacious galleries and balconies with large open shuddered windows and terra cotta tinted flagstones forming wide roomy walkways.

Gigantic century old oaks with massive gnarled branches shawled with Spanish moss swaying in the summer breezes.... sprawling green lawns trimmed with flowering hedges of glorious colors.

Delightful fragrances emitted from outlying roses, wisterias, jasmines and magnolia trees clothed in song by colorful garden birds.

Suddenly all is graced alive with ravishing Southern Belles in delicate feminine gowns of silk, satin and organdy; appearing like goddesses stepping out of statuaries carved by masterful sculptors to be escorted in pleasure by gracious noble gentlemen.

Cool refreshing drinks of lemon, lime and orange; mint juleps, aromatic rums, old fashions and demitasse coffees spiked with the finest of French cognacs.

And, the unforgetable loyal and well-mannered house boy who everybody likes!

This regal social atmosphere is stimulated into a spirited festive mood by gentlemen negro musicians of unmatched jazz talents. Musicians and guests alike were transported in noble fashion from New Orleans by riverboat.

This was the typical scene of elegant gaiety at a PLANTATION LAWN PARTY DURING THE GOLDEN ERA.

* * * * * * * *

New Orleans gave birth to jazz but contrary to popular belief it did not originate in the red-light district of Storyville. It began long before that district came into existence.

Neither did jazz musicians play only in saloons and brothels, as there were more than enough social affairs and community outings to keep the good musicians of the 1800's quite comfortable and well engaged.

They played for countless house and lawn parties, private balls, picnics, parades and innumerable fraternal socials.

It was an entire new life for musicians of jazz talents and the industry flourished with numerous greats.

Many fine aristocrats of the jazz world became immortals; Jelly Roll Norton, Bunk Johnson, Baby Dodds, King Oliver, Johnny St. Cyre, Tony Jackson, Clarence Williams, George Baquet, Kidd Ross and many many more.

The list would be endless, on into the present century of greats, including that world reknown New Orleans born "Ambassador of Jazz".... Louis Armstrong.

J DeHart

Quadroon Concubines

Call her a mistress, call her a concubine or call her a lover, but one thing was certain; toward the end of the eighteenth century and during the nineteenth century in New Orleans the mulatto (or quadroon) "wife" away from home was not just a caprice, it was a style of living for many well-to-do white men. It was a society within itself and was quite fashionable.

Only in New Orleans could this sort of institution flourish with "honor." It was an accepted custom that derived from mismatches in marriages among the wealthy white population, especially within the confines of New Orleans. There were "Mariages de Convenance," the carry over from European aristocratic customs; the union of white man and white wife as a result of their parents making that marriage so that there would be a cementing of the two fortunes. Often that contract of marriage was arranged and signed by the parents even before the young couple had ever met each other. When they did meet, each may have despised the other and distasteful relations presided over their marriage from that time, lasting sometimes for life. More often than not the girl became unhappy, tense and frigid. Atmospheres of love or sexual satisfaction could not be generated at home and to find this the husband would seek out a mistress who was capable of warmer relationships.

Everyone knew this way of life was to be accepted, even the wife was fully aware of it and faced up to that fact as though it was to be a part of life she had to become accustomed to, although she may have pretended that no such condition existed. White women of New Orleans made many attempts to degrade or humble the mulatto women and were known to have had them whipped in public using any excuse available to justify such actions. White women were even successful in having a law passed which prevented mulatto women from wearing any headdress other than a "tignon," this being a simple kerchief tied over the head. But with great talents for creating the unusual and the beautiful these mulattoes devised attractive designs for headpieces created from tignons. Regardless of what the white woman did to try to discourage the mulatto mistress it was overcome and proven ineffective.

That mistress was either mulatto or quadroon, the daughter of a white man and a mulatto woman, but for convenience sake the word mulatto was used for all, regardless of the degree of negro blood.

These women were said to be very beautiful with elegantly dignified mannerisms. They had been trained by their mothers from the cradle for a role in life as a concubine for a wealthy white "husband." White men appeared to be much more at ease in their presence, more so than when in the company of white women. Many mulatto women were far more pleasant and certainly much less critical of other women, paying more attention toward interests created between man and woman. They always made their white men very proud of them with their attentive, charming attitudes.

The quadroon girl was tutored privately and in some cases by the nuns at Ursuline. She was taught to read and write well, she was taught to sew, cook and keep house in the best of fashion. She was trained to care for herself and keep herself immaculately clean, well groomed and to dress to perfection. She was taught grace and elegance and to speak softly in a pleasant manner, and was very well schooled in the art of conversation. Her virginity was well guarded until that very day when she was finally accepted into that select society as a mistress to a white man. This level of acceptance was very much envied even by many white women who would have gladly ventured into this way of life had social standards accepted it.

The mulatto mistress was a charming and elegant hostess, even at the largest dinner or social gathering. She dressed as well as many white women of high social position. By many world travelers mulatto women were lauded as being the most beautiful in the world. To add to their natural beauty and charm they wore fine mantillas or skillfully designed headpieces, elaborate coiffures, silks, satins, velvets, plumes and gorgeous jewelry. Everything they did was directed toward a pleasant and fulfilling life with her white "husband." Very seldom did any betray the trust white men had in them.

In 1790 the population of New Orleans was eight thousand and fifteen hundred were unmarried mulatoo women either of mistress status or available for it. Even during this early period this was a flourishing profession. Many young unmarried men supported mistresses and even after his marriage to a white woman this mistress often remained in his keeping at a second home.

Should this arrangement be terminated she was usually granted a respectable settlement. Seldom did she become mistress to a second white man, because of her devotion for the first "husband" she would turn to other professions, such as milliner, dressmaker, hairdresser, etc. Many prospered in such undertakings, which was usually financed by the "ex-husband." A discarded quadroon mistress seldom ever married and if she did it was never to anyone blacker than a mulatto. Laws forbade legal marriage between a person of color and a white, if it was done neither could maintain a status of white.

Children born of a Creole man and a mulatto woman were well cared for and some were even educated in France. Young girls followed the footsteps and profession of their mothers, but young boys were less fortunate, they either married negroes or a discarded mulatto mistress who wanted to venture into marriage.

The mulatto girl, having been tutored to appreciate the arts, sought the entertainments offered by the theatre and opera, attending them often and very much in fashion. Usually it was here that she was first noticed by her potential white suitor. It was here at the theatre that her charms, beauty and grace first exploited the white male world. She arrived in regal splendor, dressed in low cut gowns of silk in vivid hues and with jewelry that accented her charms and beauty. It was here at the theatre and it was here at the opera that she created interests from a prospective "husband," inviting him to the mulatto debutant ball, widely known as the Quadroon Ball. There he and the girl could be placed in a comfortable atmosphere to discuss arrangements for their "marriage." She was presented at this ball very much in the same manner as a white debutant of high society.

The Quadroon Balls were openly advertised in the newspapers and only men of dignity and position were allowed to attend. They risked no social stigma by attending, it was very fashionable to do so.

The balls were joyful, dignified and lavish.... never ever vulgar. They even surpassed the quality of entertainment and pleasures that existed at the all white ball of high social status. The prominent male population of New Orleans indulged regularly in Quadroon Balls, it was widely favored by them. Even those with no interests in selecting a mistress would attend, they enjoyed the elegance and pleasantries that existed at these formals.

The mulatto girl did have the last word in the selection of a white "husband," for it was she who must be pleased before she could make any man happy or contented. But once she had decided to accept a particular man for a "husband" all other arrangements were carried out between the girl's mother and the man. The girl was usually awarded a home where she and her mother were to live, this in most cases was located in the outlying sections of the present day Vieux Carre on or near Rampart Street. From that time on her life as "wife" to her white "husband" was with sincere devotion on both the part of the girl and that of her mother. The mother always played the role of a consultant in selecting proper furnishings, servants and care of the home. Often she was cook and housekeeper, but more often than not they were afforded servants and had access to a carriage.

The girl lived very comfortably and her sole obligation was that of creating a happy home for her and her "husband." It was a duty to keep in perfect readiness for whenever her lover came. When he was there she saw to it that there were atmospheres of romantic pleasantries. And, she was always expected to be impeccably faithful; never ever giving the slightest reason for doubt or mistrust.

The concubine society lasted to the end of the nineteenth century; it was a fashioned lifestyle that became very much a part of the unique history of old New Orleans.

"IT'S NEVER TOO LATE"

Defend Yourself, Sir!

Dueling established itself firmly in New Orleans during the eighteenth century, but after the Louisiana Purchase in 1803 it became a mania. For almost sixty years it was a serious way of life in New Orleans, nowhere else in America was it easier to be killed.

Rapiers, pistols, rifles and shotguns were weapons chosen in dueling, but never among the elite was anyone to lower his dignity by attempting to settle an argument by the lowly art of fisticuffs.

At the drop of a handkerchief one could become offended into challenging another to a duel that more likely than not was to end in death. If a man lived in New Orleans he took it for granted that he would not go very long without a duel. Very seldom was an offense corrected by an apology alone, and reconciliation without a duel was only occasional. The least breach of etiquette, even if unintentional, could result in a duel.

Certain areas of the city were designated to serve as arenas for dueling, the Père Antoine Garden behind St. Louis Cathedral was most frequented since it was conveniently located for all parties. But, other places became popular, such as the Fortin plantation (presently the location of the fair grounds) and the Allard plantation west of Bayou St. John. The latter is now the area of the existing City Park and became the most celebrated dueling grounds in America. The huge trees with its moss covered branches trailing to the grounds was the most fashionable place of dueling ever known and brought large "galleries" to that site to view as many as twelve duels a week in the shades of the Allard Oaks.

Schools of dueling were popular, night after night fencing lessons were numerous and the ringing of steel could be heard throughout Exchange Alley from Canal to St. Louis. There were many masters who taught thousands of young male adults in the skill of using the sword. Some of those teachers were immensely popular: L'Alouette, Alsatian, Lebourette, Thimecourt, Dauphin, Bonneval, Llulla and others. But, master of masters was one Gilbert Rosiere, a youth from Bordeaux, France who had come to America to study law and had become, instead, the most able and the richest of all New Orleans' fencing masters. He was a man of many good tastes and enjoyed the theatre, the opera, fine music, exquisite foods, good wines and well-bred ladies of culture. He was the idol of all, men and women alike.

To be a famous "maitre d'armes" during that period of valor was to enjoy such glories bestowed upon great matinee idols and celebrated military heroes.

J De Hart

Possessed Souls

Summer evenings were bathed with the refreshing lake breezes at the commencement of the *Voodoo rituals* on the shores of Bayou St. John. Hundreds of blacks, whites and those of intermingled blood participated in those eventful gatherings. Ceremonies were primitive and lustful with sadistic overtones. Theirs was to delight their *"Papa La Bas,"* king of devils and ruler of serpents.

Dozens of blazing torches encircle vast clearings at the bayou's edge; centered is a huge caldron of *"Voodoo gumbo"* and a sacrificial altar with seven black glimmering candles. Their high priestess presides with a bewitching dominance. Standing on the box of her sacred *zombi* she raises the huge serpent over her shoulders enticing it into kissing her cheek.... thus his sanctions to begin the cermonies.

As always, fruit, *"congris,"* a bowl of goat blood and seven silver coins in toast to their supreme ruler. Into the caldron she tosses live chickens, frogs, snails and always a sacrificial snake divided into three equal pieces, suggesting a diabolic trinity. In communion, all partake of the gumbo, warm blood and stimulating *"tafia"*....the rituals now begin with the sounding of a great conch seashell.

The *Calinda* and the *Bamboula,* set into wild tempos by primtive congo drums, create atmospheres of *"affaires d'armour."* Servings of steaming love potions enhance the effects of the tafia and inflame passions for erotic dance. Their priestess is clothed in a gown of fifty red handkerchiefs so stitched to suggestively wrap her body. Beneath a seven pointed tignon her lustrous long ebony tresses hang down below her waist; large gold earrings caresse the lobes of her shell-shaped ears while glowing candlelight dances shimmering highlights upon her moist black skin. She moves with the captivating grace of an enchanting viper. Her hypnotic eyes sparkle as she drinks from the bowl of blood and decanter of tafia.... she extends generous portions to her devoted followers. She is the essence of the voodoos in that orgastic world of unchaste morals and blackened magic.

These are the bizarre voodooistic practices dominated by lecherous women intoxicated with the mythical powers granted to them by their satanic ruler. Powers that contaminate souls of healthy bodies with weak minds, bringing them into mystical atmospheres of total submission.

Bonfires blaze, drums take up a beat and naked men dance with flaming torches and plates of ignited alcohol; the spinning, gyrating and leaping increasing in tempos with the hastening cadence of the Bamboula drums. Black muscled flesh glisten with sweat as the slow measured dance begins to accelerate. They chant out congo songs to the quickened beat of the tom-toms while deafening screams pierce from the throats of the possessed.

Adorned with charms, beads and magical bells, women rip off their clothes while slithering serpents entwine themselves onto their nude bodies so stimulated into passionate rhythms by rum and incensed candles. Yellow, white and black girls dance together while others reach into the darkness for their male lovers. They become sadistically obsessed; clawing, biting and scratching they draw blood in barbaric fashions. Drums grow fiercely louder while flickering candles suddenly glow into blinding balls of fire; ....then as if drawing a last breath of life, torches dim, then submit to total darkness.

....Clouds break and the full moon casts eerie glows upon naked bodies that had fallen to the earth in pairs. The night is silenced in darkness leaving only waning candlelights and faint flickering embers of the dying bonfires.

Soon they arouse to cleanse their bodies in the refreshing bayou waters.... in a while their unchaste souls will again become intoxicated with frenzied lust and with unrestrained passions crave for another spiritual intercourse with satan.... *once again they become totally possessed and submit to the wicked wishes of the "Papa La Bas."*

* * * * * * * *

Although those evening rituals and orgies were often frightful and sadistic they were just small segments of the voodoo culture. Voodooism was a religion for many who indulged in sorcery on everyday basis to the extent of obsessive fanaticism. In Louisiana it was a living and breathing thing to those people and they practiced it with a passion for over two centuries.

Voodooism was brought into Louisiana from Africa by slaves in the early seventeen hundreds and it became very prevalent throughout southern Louisiana, especially in New Orleans. Although it was outlawed by the state some plantation negroes did indulge in voodooism, but it was most active in towns and cities where communications, secret gatherings and voodoo exercises were easier to accomplish.

Women made up about eighty percent of the cult's activities and a number of the members were white women who often participated in rituals where *Fe Chauffé* dances were performed at Lake Ponchartrain. Some white men went to those events, but mainly to make contact with yellow-skin girls for sexual engagements.

Voodoo powers were most effective among negroes and were especially successful on minds easily influenced and susceptive to suggestion.

The Priestess or Queen ruled the cult, kings were only minor figures. Most powerful and successful of all queens was Marie Laveau who reigned in New Orleans for the better part of the 1800's; voodooism thrived under her regime. After her death cult activities began to decline from lack of leadership. As negroes became more educated Christianity soon replaced their spiritual needs for voodoosim.

The Devil Made Her Do It!

The "Voodoo" came here from Africa
in seventeen twenty-four,
and started up the strangest cult
like no one's seen before

For seventy years in the eighteen hundreds
their queen was Marie Laveau,
the most feared of them all
who put on quite a show.

She'd cook up a drink of "healing powers"
with turtles, frogs and lizards,
and to conjure up "make sick" potions
she'd add some chicken gizzards.

Three XXX's marked down on the banquette
meant this house was under gris-gris
and was held by evil spirits
with no chance of getting free.

There was a gris-gris to make you ill
and a gris-gris to get you well,
a hex for this, a hex for that
and a hex to send you to hell.

She'd sell some bags of colored sand
to drive away bad spirits,
or did a lot of "hoodoo" stuff
to scare you out of your wits.

She made plenty o' chanting noises
which was just mumbo-jumgo,
and most of all her "magic" potions
were simply filé gumbo.

There was lots of money that she made
just playing on their minds,
for those who believed all that stuff
were the weak and naive kind.

Continued . . . .

T'was said before she passed away
she'd come back from the dead,
to forever be their ruler
and keep those people scared.

Well, that really hasn't happened
and her stories often vary,
but as far as everyone knows
she's in St. Louis Cemetery.

So you wipe away all of those fears
and fret not the days of old,
you can bet your bottom dollar
the Devil's done got her soul.

EARLY ACADIAN MAIDEN

AMANTS DE MARDI GRAS

Mardi Gras

This display of magic and madness acted out on the stages of historic New Orleans is complete with an audience of millions and a cast in the hundreds of thousands. It is the greatest free show on earth. There are guests from all walks of life, from any land on earth.

This "great pretense" has become a cult with memberships increasing in vast numbers every year. Its members could be Donald Duck, Mickey Mouse, a long-necked giraffe, a female impersonator, a pirate, a vagabond, or hundreds of other characters. It's a fabulous thousand ring circus with maskers, parades, balls, private soirees and a street party like nowhere else on earth. The season can be as few as twenty-eight days and as many as sixty-three, depending on the date of Easter Sunday; Mardi Gras season is measured from January sixth through Shrove Tuesday (day before Ash Wednesday).

Early resemblance to Mardi Gras can be traced as far back as five thousand years, when Arcadian sheperds of Greece celebrated the coming of Spring by sacrificing goats, feasting on the flesh, then making whips from the skin for painted and blood bathed priests to lash naked men and women in sadistic and depraved celebrations throughout the streets of their villages. The first maskers of these known celebrations were female impersonators who preyed on other men for sexual adventures. It was an accepted festival of fertility when even women of social position donned costumes and masks and prostituted themselves for pleasures of the flesh to strangers of both sexes. This festival of feasts and orgies was practiced by all, kings and commoners alike.

With the coming of Christianity this celebration of heathens was overwhelmingly condemned as paganistic and sinful. That season of immoral ceremony was then transformed into events of dignified fasting and abstinence from earthly pleasures of the body. But, in spite of this change through Christianity some of the heathenish practices remained through the years and the Christian leaders were powerless in their attempts to correct it, even with the strict bans placed on such depraved behaviors.

This season of feasts and festivals was further adopted by the Romans and then passed onto the French. And, when the first French settlers came to Louisiana they brought with them this ancient custom. Further adjustments followed over the years, creating this unique festive tradition experienced only in Louisiana.

To further justify the need for such enjoyment, early Louisiana settlers who were faced with many devastating floods, hurricanes, plagues, offensive winters and summers, fires, famine and many other depressing hardships found it absolutely essential to create situations that would boost their spirits and give to them periods and atmospheres of gaiety to get their minds off the past and oncoming hard-to-bear discomforts. They felt that this was necessary in order to maintain their own sanity during the coming hot humid summers plagued with mosquitoes and fevers. For months they were forced to stay indoors with minimum social activities because of those conditions.

The first Mardi Gras in Louisiana was celebrated on Shrove Tuesday, March 3, 1699, thirty miles upriver from the mouth of the Mississippi when Iberville staked a claim on lands of Louisiana in the name of the King of France. He and a handful of men celebrated Mardi Gras on a bleak piece of land along the great river, that piece of soil was then named Mardi Gras Point. It wasn't too many years after that when early settlers celebrated Fat Tuesday with soirees (informal balls) and festive gatherings.

The first formal ball was held in New Orleans in 1743 by the governor, Marquis de Vaudreuil. This marked the beginning of yearly celebrations with elaborate balls throughout the carnival season. Parades and street masking along with many private parties and street revelers were added through the years.

Krewes (social Mardi Gras clubs) were organized and in 1820 when tableaus were created for the balls, establishing a custom for all formal socials thereafter. Street masking on Mardi Gras in New Orleans began when people first started masquerading for those balls and traveled to and from on the streets, often numbering into the hundreds. Inevitability this led to great street parties, some of the revelers never arriving at the intended balls.

The first organized parade was formed by the Krewe of Comus in 1837; this was the Krewe that brought such good taste and drama to the balls and also created the first night parade in 1857. Flambeau lights illuminated the colorful floats and touched off a trend never to end. In 1884 Comus gave Mardi Gras its first queen, Mildred Lee, daughter of the beloved Confederate General Robert E. Lee. Her court included such notables as Varina Davis, daughter of Confederate President Jefferson Davis, May Lee, another daughter of the General and Julia Jackson, daughter of General Stonewall Jackson. Prior to this only kings reigned over Mardi Gras events.

Rex and Momus emerged in 1872 with fabulous parades and formals. It was in that year Rex was crowned King of Mardi Gras and has held that distinctive title ever since. Other Mystick Krewes were later formed, parades added and the Mardi Gras season grew more spectacular every year with greater celebrations and more elaborate costumes.

The custom of "throws" from floats began in 1871. The Twelfth Night Revelers parade had for its theme "Mother Goose Rhymes," and in it was Santa Claus. This jolly old gentleman had trinkets that he dug out of his bag and threw to the crowds. Although these were only cheap ornaments it created such excitement that it was forever afterwards adopted by float riders in all parades. And, the great doubloon stampede began in 1960 when the Krewe of Rex minted the first such throw that has been a popular item not only for parades but it also added the new dimension of doubloon collecting.

Colorful jazz bands were the first to furnish music for parades but with the coming of musician's unions the jazz bands priced themselves right out of jobs with high fees and were replaced by high school and college bands who were more than eager to display their musical talents to such vast audiences.

Mardi Gras season actually begins January sixth, the Twelfth Night of Christmas, the day the Magi brought gifts to infant Jesus. Celebrations for the carnival season gains in momentum from that day through Fat Tuesday when the climax is reached with more gaiety, more celebrating, more feasting than is experienced anywhere else in the world.

Romantic New Orleans loves her Mardi Gras and the carnival fever begins to rise even before the New Year arrives. But for twelve months of the year, in secrecy, Krewes are at work creating themes, floats, costumes and fascinating scenes for the season to come. Thousands are employed in many facets of this industry that is solely privately financed. Yet, it generates a multi-million dollar business to the city's economy and has become one of America's greatest tourist attractions.

Employment is furnished year round to costume designers, souvenir makers, caterers, seamstresses, musicians, hotel-motel establishments, importers and many many others. Because of carnival season and its many parties and balls, more formal wear is sold in New Orleans than any other city in America.... this includes New York City. The scope of this unique industry is unbelievably endless. It attracts visitors by the millions each season and establishes tourist interests throughout the year, an industry that has become second only to the Port of New Orleans in all of Louisiana.

Mardi Gras is a time when the ditch digger can become a king, the cleaning woman a queen and a little orphan girl becomes a princess. It's a season of skimpy costumes on pretty girls, a dignified matron from the "garden district" dresses like a chamber maid and entire families are costumed like indians or clowns. It's the Zulu parade with a witch doctor who has the "Big Shot" and African warriors with spears and skirts of grass.

It's children and adults alike shouting "throw me something mister." The actors of this great theatre of comedy and festive drama can become on Mardi Gras Day anything that he or she may wish to be.

Many have attempted to write and describe to others what Mardi Gras is really like.... and as many have failed to do so. It is impossible to do this, an understanding of it can only be had by those who come to experience it first hand. Even then, they may want a second or third visit so that they may try to fulfill the needs of cravings generated during this great festive season.

MARTY GRAW ©

J DeHart

Phantasyland, U.S.A.

Wake up.....................!!
Wake up to the sounds of revelers
who are celebrating Mardi Gras,
Lent will be here tomorrow......
so be it, this, your last hurrah!
LADY NEW ORLEANS is under the spell
of that great carnival fever,
Seems like all America came to visit
and doesn't want to leave her!
It isn't a time for just the kids
playing like grown-ups for a day,
The grown-ups have loads of fun
just acting in a childish way.

Rex, he's the King of Mardi Gras
Proteus, "the old man of the sea,"
Comus, is the eldest of them all
but ZEUS....who in the heck is he?
Fantastic parades with beautiful floats
and marchers with flaming flambeaus,
Magnificent balls and outdoor parties
and many great tableaus.
There's the Princess and the Duchess
and Prince, Counts, Dukes and Earls,
There's many different Sheiks about
with dozens of Harem Girls.

Yes, this is a FANTASY LAND
where each is someone else,
The only day throughout the year
you need not be yourself.
This can be that very time
the Harlot can be a Nun
And a Priest becomes quite Devilish
just to have a bit of fun.
There'll be many Cops and Robbers
when the Banker becomes a Clown,
A Housewife is a teasing Strumpet
the Jezebel of the town.

Continued . . . .

A pretty girl comes quite undressed
in a very skimpy costume,
With so very little that's left
for people to presume.
And, she who looks like Joan of Arc
is a French Quarter Stripper,
Yes, her "costume" is no disguise
she's like that to sell some liquor.
There are many different kinds of Queens
to be seen around the town,
Some are "men" that's rather queer
other, real ladies who wear the crowns.

Visitors come here by the thousands
to fill the Vieux Carré,
Jamming coffee houses and saloons
in a gay and festive way.
The "Old Town" is quite alive
with different kinds of bands,
Those who play while on the march
while others are "DIXIELAND."
It's a great display of magic
when trinkets are thrown about,
Turning the streets into a madness
along the parading route.

There's a series of performing stages
set about the New Orleans town
The multitudes become the actors
while the stars just lay around.
The greatest free show of them all
is acted out upon the streets,
A circus of a thousand rings
grandest of all the feats!

And, the disposition of the people
is as carefree as you ever saw........
"The whole world must wait until tomorrow,
for today is MARDI GRAS!"

VENTURES ON LOUISIANA WATERS

The Mississippi River Of The 1800's

In the manner of a gigantic serpent, the great Father of American waters winds its way through this country's heartland bringing lifebloods and economic wealth into countless communities and numerous plantations. With its many tributaries, no other single stream has ever controlled so many lives or so many fortunes. In all its glory it has carved into American soils cultures never seen or experienced anywhere else. Its numerous affluents reach out easterly and reach out westerly to funnel great wealths into the vast farmsteads of ancient Louisiana.

Upon its surface glide scores of vessels of every description. There are paddle-wheel steamboats loaded with hogsheads of sugar and bales of cotton from farmland kingdoms. There are packets for carrying mail and passengers to various and distant ports. There are floating hotels for luxurious travel and there is the gay and delightful showboat with actors, dancers and singers entertaining at a different landing every night. There are numerous varieties of barges, flatboats, rafts, keelboats and schooners milling their way to and from large and tiny ports that dot the shorelines from St. Louis to New Orleans; with cargos of leather, furs, dress fabrics, home furnishings and multitudes of other products.

A stew of humanity from all banquettes of life swarm over every deck, every gangplank and into every port. From the common riverside vagabond to the gallant prince from foreign lands, all are bewitched by the captivating mysteries of Father Mississippi. Wealthy merchants and planters journey upon these waters anxious to visit great ports like Memphis and New Orleans, to frolic in swank coffee houses, gambling palaces and lavish bordellos. Boisterous boatmen converge profanely upon cheap barrooms, dives and lowly brothels of Natchez-Under-The-Hill. Elements from every land and from every nation is lured by the excitements and hypnotic charms of Old Man River.

Upon the green shoulders of either shore there is a magnitude of interesting levee people. There are wooding stations for steamboats, docking platforms filled with bales of cotton and tobacco and multitudes of negro workers hastily trying to avert a disastrous crevasse. A hearty old darky waves a white cloth to hail an approaching packet while nearby stands his master with a valise enroute to Baton Rouge. In a distance, beyond that neat row of pink crepe mrytles, patrician gentlemen and beautifully gowned ladies gather upon the verandah of a pillared mansion; tuneful melodies drift with the light breezes; perhaps a wedding, perhaps an evening party. The river brought everything and everyone to them, the river will take everyone and everything away.

Trimmed with many ornaments from nature; seagulls, egrets, reptiles and numerous other creatures of the wild, the ancient Mississippi breathes life into all living things. And too.... it has taken away many lives into the treacherous depths of its violent waters. Catastrophic explosions of steamboat boilers were often, disastrous fires and sinkings of vessels were frequent. Terrifying crevasses engulf land and dwellings and there are constant fears of violence created by brutal men who travel these milk chocolate waters. Human saddness and tragic events have often quelled gay atmospheres of merriment.

This magnificent but fickle old Mississippi with all its romantic intrigue has changed its mind and its direction so many times it could well bear the title "Lady" of American waters. But, it has won admiration and love from around the world. This is a giant who has gained a grandeur of affection from millions of American hearts.

Those are the images of a "Great River" of the eighteen hundreds which are engraved into the minds of modern man.

Floating Palaces

Rhythmic strokes of the paddle wheel, towering smokestacks belching black clouds and the lustrous brass calliope echoing melodious tunes of gaiety. Sumptuous vessels with delightfully decorated arches, fretted scrolls, brilliant blazes of gilt and glittering crystal chandeliers; elegant staterooms and magnificent salons. Elaborate dining rooms with the finest linens, exquisite china, shining silver, sparkling cut glass and menus that are paralleled only by the magnificent restaurants of old New Orleans.

This, the most loved adventure that America has ever produced had romance in every cabin, at every dining table and on every promenade. Floating palaces with marvelous paintings, outstanding sculptures, beautiful plush carpets and fabulously carved furniture. Crowds of gay proud people flooded the decks, dining halls and salons; distinguished merchants and wealthy planters, stylish ladies and noble gentlemen, colorful personalities of the stage and reknown figures of tasteful cultures.

Stern-wheeler or side-wheeler, those elegant steamboats gave to the people pleasures and excitements never ever again to be matched. Thrilling experiences in quaint cities along the rivers and bayous, breathtaking scenery on shores, splendid waterways busied by hundreds of bewitching vessels and interesting people; charming ship masters, talented chefs and gracious stewards. Suave and cunning gamblers, rowdy roustabouts and multitudes of curious levee dwellers. Cherished memories of the great river enhanced by fabulous mansions with stately white pillars.

Those fascinating aqua-queens dominated the rivers and bayous, gliding over the waters surface with the grace and charm of exotic dancing girls seducing their subjects with intriguing adventures, dazzling luxuries, superb comforts and entertainments unsurpassed. They are not myths, they are not imaginary symbols of America, they are factual living legends never to be erased from our sacred heritage. They are America of the yesteryears, they are America of today and after nearly two hundred years of reign they continue to prevail in the enchanting bayou lands of ancient Louisiana with the glamour and splendor of an immortal goddess.

J DeHart

Legend Of The Vagabond Ship

The early autumn sun bathed the "Joli Demoiselle" in warmth. Her white sails were swelled with pride as the gallant French ship made its way through Berwick Bay toward the mouth of the ancient Atchafalaya. Captain Jacque Dubois stood proudly at the helm, casting tender glances at his lovely Francine leaning against the railing, gazing in curious peace at the strange shores in the distance; her golden tresses waved gently in the breezes. He had taken his beloved with him for a rare and exciting adventure into a new world far from her native France. Cheerful passengers eager to return to their Techeland homes with tales of exciting months in Bordeau, Rouen, Lyon and Paris filled the decks with joyous ecstasy. Their long journey was near its end.

There were owners of great farmsteads, wives and daughters of noble planters and wealthy merchants, and there were student sons from Gallic colleges returning for duties as plantation managers. An aristocratic French couple with their two children voyaging for a winter visit to Petit Paris (St. Martinville) were so anxious to once again see their loving Louisiana relations. In the ship's hold there were treasures of fine linens and silks for the home or personal wear, there were silver and gold furnishings, and there were costly gifts for loved ones unable to travel with them. All were well and very thankful for a voyage without mishap or illness.... weary seamen sighed in relief.

They were so excited and happy that most were unaware of the sudden strange calming of the winds and quieting of the channel's turbulent waters. Bellowing sails became still, without swell, and mast top banners hung limp. The vessel was soon without motion, then came curious whisperings as the silence became disturbing. Soaring sea gulls burst forth into screaming choruses of rage as if violently attacked by monstrous winged predators. The sun's rays turned cold and gray and a frightening aura of desolation settled over the vessel, fear shrouded the joy of just a short while ago. Women sought the embrace of men and children whimpered as they grasped the protective hands of their elders.... Francine turned to Jacque and began to slowly move toward him.

Then suddenly!.... Boisterous bellowing commands from Captain Dubois broke this ghostly silence! His trained senses of many years at sea had warned him of oncoming dangers. Seamen were sent scampering up ratlines in desperate attempts to lower sails. "Seal the hatches! All passengers go midship! Down to the deck!...." on and on he shouted forceful commands in frenzied efforts to safeguard the vessel and her travelers. Without warning, skies became blackened by fierce enormous clouds and winds burst forth into devastating speeds while waves reached high to lick the decks with monstrous watery tongues. The ship tossed and twisted violently swaying tall masts back and forth, pitching veteran mariners upon terrified passengers below while the raging waters engulfed them into its belly.

Lashing himself to the helm, Jacque reached out in desperation for his lovely Francine as she frantically made her way toward his outstretched arms. Then, only inches away from his grasp, a tremendous wave sent her screaming into the blackened depths of the bay.

For endless hours savage winds howled and screamed while violent waters raced furiously across the lifeless decks of the valiant craft. Debris was hurled in every direction and upon helpless bodies afloat. Torrential rains and winds churned the sea with horrifying fury, removing all hopes of survival for any who were still alive.

Then.... the dawn of the morning to follow brought once again that frightening stillness that had shrouded the "Joli Demoiselle" the afternoon before. All her passengers and crew were lost into treacherous waters; her captain lay motionless beneath the wheel, still lashed to its staff. Once again there was a strange and eerie silence broken only by shrills of returning gulls and the perpetual knell of the ship's bell, as though they were singing out a eulogy of those resting souls who had vanished into the darkened depths of this now tranquil sea.

A century and one-half has now passed since that horrifying nightmare on Berwick Bay, but tales are still heard from many who venture into those mysterious waters, tales by some who, in the wake of violent storms, have seen the "Joli Demoiselle" with her tattered sails and dangling lines drifting aimlessly about in mystical fashion. Her brave Captain still at her helm searching hopefully for his delicate little mistress who had been swept away so helplessly into that dark and dreadful night. Some have seen him with lantern in hand moving about in shiftless silence, first to the port side, then starboard and back to the helm. Others have heard the faint mournful cries of a young lady, as if whimpering in distressful loneliness; while begging the helpful hand of her distraught lover.

....Will sorrows of that tragic happening continue to haunt in eternal fashion? ....Will memories of that fateful event of horrors prolong endless tortures to the aching heart of this courageous skipper as his vagabond sailship drifts into and out of the misty shadows of a foggy bay?.... Or.... perhaps an equally devastating force of nature will finally bring an end to his sad and fruitless search by mercifully casting him into spiritual wedlock with the soul of his beloved Francine, bringing blissful silence to the mournful tolling of that ancient nautical bell which has brought so much sadness into the hearts of all lovers.

LONE SURVIVOR

Silent sounds from the paddle wheel mingled with the still of a peaceful night. All were bedded down for the voyage that many had taken with her on the mighty Mississippi. She was the riverboat *"La Belle Creole,"* that gallant lady of delightful journeys.

Before complete slumber was to come, one lovely maiden was still awake preparing the refreshing scented waters for her bath. Alone in her cabin near that of her loved ones, she felt so very much at peace; with love.

Then suddenly, breaking that beautiful silence, from below came terrifying rumbles and belching of the boilers! La Belle Creole had come alive! With sputtering jets of steam shooting from her insides she burst into flames and torrid explosions tore vast holes into her decks and gutted her staterooms! Sleeping bodies were strewn hundreds of feet into the cold dreadful waters and debris from the decks was sprinkled upon them!

Then, quietly again, there was a silent darkness; but not so beautiful. La Belle Creole had come to her end into the awesome depths of the mighty Mississippi.... a stupefying calm shrouded the air in sadness.

One was alive, and like a giant arm of salvation came the mast of the "Belle" to lift her afloat and to the edge of the darkened waters. She was *"The Lone Survivor"* of the mass wreckage and nightmare of deaths that had come into that peaceful night. She was Charlene André standing stunned, naked and alone on the bank of the river. Her only remaining possessions; a locket bearing pictures of her loved ones and the flag from La Belle Creole for her clothing.

PADDLE WHEEL

A Remnant Of The Past

If it could be told such stories it would tell,
the old stern-wheel from the riverboat.

Perhaps a trip with gayly decked crowds
headed for someplace remote,
Or a minstrel show on Bayou Teche
with actors from Norfolk.

It may relate stories of Berwick Bay
that would goose bump your spine,
Or tell you of a hazardous trip
down the mighty Mississippi line.

Would it sing songs of happier days
when passengers were plenty,
And forget how so often times
that tragedies were many?

It might tell you of its captains
the true gentlemen with pride,
Or the one of scruples few
and vices he could not hide.

Of the many ports and docks
it berthed while on its trips,
And tales ever so romantic
visioned with mystical ships.

Could it tell you of its cargoes
of cotton, furs and hides,
Or remember that great event
it raced the river with pride?

But, it only stands there in silence
a proud and noble outcast
With weathered paddles and rusted bolts
just a remnant of the past.

J DeHart

Jean Laffite's Baratarian's

Jean Lafitte was popular and daring, he was a man of adventure, he was a man who sought out dangers and he was a man who thrived on risking his life for the sake of the underdog.

An expert with the foils and the pistol Jean was over six feet tall, slim, well built and was considered very handsome. His black wavy hair became prematurely gray by the time he was forty years of age. His classic profile, sparkling eyes, healthy teeth and quick witted charms attracted both men and women. Of good culture, he patronized the opera and frequented many socials; New Orleans' quadroon balls were a favorite of his.

Jean Laffite was born on April 22, 1782 of French-Spanish parents at Port-au-Prince, Santo Domingo, in that part of the West Indies now known as Haiti. He was the youngest of five brothers.... he had three sisters. In 1803, when he was twenty-two years of age, Jean and his brother, Pierre, came to New Orleans and were immediately successful as city representatives for smuggled goods of Baratarian Corsairs. Around 1810, when rival pirate groups began to disagree and create conflicts, Jean and Pierre intervened and took over leadership of the combined units, forming one of the largest and strongest army of pirates ever to travel the waterways of the world.

Jean weathered the storms of battle in the open Gulf, he overcame challenges to his command of the Baratarians and he survived triumphantly the social besets that confronted him in New Orleans. Although Jean and Pierre were men of many possessions during the early years of 1800 they lived very modestly in a dwelling at the corner of Bourbon and St. Phillip streets. On St. Phillip Street was their forge and workshop, a disguise business to cover their smuggling operations in New Orleans. All meetings and transactions pertaining to the business of contraband and slave trading took place at this dwelling on Bourbon and St. Phillip. Other shops on Royal and Chartres streets served as outlets for smuggled merchandise.

Marie Villars, Pierre's quadroon mistress living with them at the New Orleans' dwelling, looked after the household for both men. In early days in New Orleans Jean was a free spirited man who left himself available for adventure and business opportunities. But in later years he acquired a beautiful young quadroon mistress of his own who loved him with great devotion. Her name was Catherine Villars, the younger sister to Pierre's mistress.

Early in 1811, shortly after he became leader of the Baratarians, Jean built a house on Grande Terre where he and Catherine made their home. Pierre and Marie also moved to a house of their own on Grande Terre Island. The brothers continued to maintain the Bourbon and St. Phillip residence to serve as a secret meeting place for business dealings in New Orleans with the Royal and Chartres street stores still serving as outlet for contraband merchandise. Jean's first wife, Christina Levine Laffite, had died from childbirth of a daughter, Denise Jeanette, in 1804. The daughter was cared for by various foster parents until in her late teens when she went to live with her father on Grand Terre Island.

Nestled among dense groves of oranges and gnarled oaks, Jean's home on Grande Terre was the largest on the island, elegantly furnished with rich carpets, silver, glassware and many other fine items taken from Spanish ship raids.

Grand Terre Island, Grand Isle and Barataria country became a kingdom ruled by the Laffites. They bestowed princely hospitalities to those who visited them either on business or for social pleasures, whether that visitor be a dignitary, businessman or friend.

Baratarian country comprised an area of lands surrounding Barataria Bay situated about forty miles south of New Orleans near the Gulf of Mexico. Grande Terre Island and Grand Isle were the major strongholds and were highly populated with pirates and other seamen who had settled those communities to form a center for their buccaneering operations.

Laffite's most trusted lieutenant was Dominque You who was said to be another brother, but there were never any documents found to verify this. Other leaders were Beluche, Nez Coupé and Gambi; Gambi being very troublesome in the early years of Laffite's leadership. It was because of this Gambi in the first place that the Baratarians found it necessary to seek out the Laffite's leadership.

The Baratarians attacked mainly Spanish ships, taking from them many prizes in gold, silk and furnishings along with Negro slaves that were being shipped to New Orleans as laborers for plantations and merchants. Many Spanish women were taken captive to serve as mistresses for Baratarian men. Racial blends in Barataria country consisted mainly of French, Spanish and Portugeuse. A number of their women were from New Orleans, Techeland and Lafourche country. Some were French Creoles, others were mulattoes and quadroons. A few were there voluntarily for the excitement and adventure, but many were kidnapped and forced to live on the islands against their wishes.

Until Jean became their leader the pirates from Barataria were quite troublesome to city guards (police) of New Orleans when they were in town. They fought in free-for-alls, tramped through muddy streets late at night, drunk, singing loud songs and shouting obscenities. They were known to climb balconies to kidnap the women of local merchants, but after taking over leadership Laffite forbade such behaviors and quickly disciplined offenders. However, when kidnapped women were given the opportunity to return to New Orleans none were ever known to do so.... reasons unknown. Perhaps pleasure, adventure and excitements kept them there. Or, perhaps it was the probable shame and scandal that would bring to them a dishonor they knew they could not live with in a society of such scrutiny.

Laffite's warehouses of goods on Grande Terre Island and on Grand Isle overflowed with valuable merchandise of contraband and was regularly shipped to New Orleans to sell at prices below that of local merchants. There were also many auctions of prize goods held at the "Temple," an ancient Indian mound of white shell in the midst of beautiful old oaks on Bayou Barataria. Also, many convoys of small boats were sent to Bayou Lafourche and Teche country trading posts to sell their rich prizes to French farmers and small town merchants.

Smuggling wasn't their only means of livelihood, many of the Baratarians were expert hunters, trappers and fishermen who sold their catches, furs and meats to the markets of New Orleans.

During the Battle of New Orleans, Baratarians led by Jean, Pierre and Dominque You courageously fought the British alongside the forces of General Andrew Jackson. High honors and letters of credit were given to them by their one-time enemies, Governor Claiborne and General Jackson, stating that without the Baratarians New Orleans and Louisiana may have easily been lost to the British. Had New Orleans gone down in defeat the entire structure of Louisiana society could have easily been altered, and could have drastically changed this unique heritage which has been preserved in great part by the unselfish courage of those unforgetable noble corsairs of Barataria country.

* * * * * * * *

History records reflect that in his later years, under the alias of John Lafflin, Jean moved to Baltimore and invested in the shipping business. His second marriage (when he was fifty years of age) was to Emma Hortense Mortimore, a beautiful twenty-three year old Charleston, South Carolina girl. She bore him two sons, Jules Jean and Glen Hénri. He lived out most of his later years in Baltimore, but his last home was in Alton, Illinois.

One day in May, when learning of the illness of a friend and his wife at their farm ten miles away, Jean journeyed through the cold rain to aid them. Finding them in dire need of food Jean sought out in cold drizzling rain to gather edibles. To keep their home warm he had also gone out into the cold rain to chop wood, not just for their immediate needs, but he cut an ample supply for their future use. Only when he was sure that their comforts for some time would be satisfied did he return home.

That prolonged exposure to the cold soaking rain under extreme physical exertion brought on to him the deadly grip of pneumonia.... at seventy-two years of age, on Friday, May 5, 1854, in his home at Alton, Illinois, Jean Laffite died peacefully in the arms of his beloved wife Emma.

NOTE: Repeatedly, time after time, Laffite's name has been spelled with one "f" and two "t's" [Lafitte] and over the years this spelling has become common in use. The author has chosen to spell it just as Jean Laffite himself wrote it. His ship's manifests along with letters by Jean shows his signature spelled as it is written in this book.

Louisiana's Hidden Treasures

There are records of many treasures in gold, silver or other prizes that were hidden or buried in Louisiana; treasures of wealthy planters, businessmen, pirates and privateers. The following shows some that have been located as well as others yet to be uncovered.

RECOVERED TREASURES

NEW ORLEANS	1915 - 1,500 gold doubloons in the heart of metropolitan New Orleans (approximately $24,000).
NEW ORLEANS	1960-outskirts of city, undetermined amount.
GRETNA	1890 - $3,000.
GRETNA	$65,000 (no date given).
COVINGTON	$10,000 within the walls of old mansion (no date).
BATON ROUGE	Gold, silver and jewels in an old cemetery (no date).
VINTON	A pirate ship on the bed of Old River near Nibletts Bluff (no date given).
PEARL RIVER	Large quantities in silver and gold on Honey Island (no date).
CAILLOU ISLAND	1851 - $2,000 in gold.
PECAN ISLAND	1925 - undetermined amount of gold and silver.
COCO ISLAND	$1,500 in gold doubloons (no date).
BUNKIE	$10,000 and 3,000 pieces of silver in a corn field (no date).
JEFFERSON ISLAND	1925 - 1,754 old coins, 2 pots of gold.
RUSTON	1,000 Spanish coins in a vacant lot (no date).
WATERPROOF	3,000 gold doubloons (approximately $48,000) buried by Quantrill (no date).
AVOYELLES PARISH	1930 - 1,000 pieces of silver plowed up by a farmer. 1939 - treasure chest in a field.
ABBEVILLE	Two gold antique vases (no date given).
CALCASIEU PARISH	1866 - $75,000 found just below a river bed. Believed to be one of Laffite's treasures.
PLAQUEMINE PARISH	$160,000 near Fort de la Boulaye, 1/2 mile north of Phoenix (no date given).
GRAND ISLAND	$1,600,000 in Spanish gold, near Caminada Pass (no date given).
BARATARIA BAY	$3,400 in gold, silver and jewels. Pure silver statue of Blessed Virgin Mary (no date given).
VERMILLION BAY	1980 - hundreds of thousands in gold, silver and other articles in 1700 Spanish galleon. Exact amounts not known.
NEW ORLEANS	1982 - large undetermined amount of Spanish doubloons, Mexican and French coins dating to early 1700's uncovered at the construction site of Meridian Hotel in downtown New Orleans.

TREASURES NOT YET UNCOVERED

PARLANGE PLANTATION	$300,000 buried when Union soldiers raided the area during the Civil War.
BATON ROUGE	$500,000 buried in an old cemetery.
VINTON	One of Jean Lafitte's ships, in Old River near Sabine River.
GALVEZ TOWN	$1,600,000 in gold in Amite River near Oak Grove.
TCHEFUNCTA RIVER	Sunken ship at the mouth near Lake Ponchartrain.
HONEY ISLAND	$2,000,000 in gold near the Pearl River.
LAKE BORGNE	$500,000 in gold, Laffite treasure on uncharted island.
COCO ISLAND	$1,000,000 in pure gold ingots.
LAKE PONCHARTRAIN	1810 - a skiff loaded with $1,725,000 of Jean Laffite's gold was sunk and never found.
MADISONVILLE	$500,000 in gold.
LINCEUM	Undetermined amount of gold dust buried.
TENSAS PARISH	Wagon filled with gold belonging to Col. Norman Fisby was overturned in Tensas River and never recovered. Location map in old Bible also lost.
ST. JAMES	$500,000 in gold and silver, near the home of a wealthy resident.
GRAND COTEAU	$3,000 in jewels, in a plantation garden hidden during the Civil War.
SELMA	$250,000 in gold dust buried in the town.
OUACHITA PARISH	$180,000 in gold, silver and jewels. Buried in an old camp during Civil War.
IN THE RIGOLETS	$270,000 in gold coins, hidden by escaped British soldiers during Battle of New Orleans, near Fort Pike.
CATOUCHE BAYOU	$240,000 in gold and silver, hidden by Jean Laffite as stated on a map in an old letter written in French.
CALCASIEU PARISH	Jayhawkers gold, buried in a swamp during the Civil War.
BRETON ISLAND	(Offshore Plaquemine's Parish) $750,000 in gold, pirate's treasure.
FORT MC COMB	1825, undetermined amounts in gold (originally this was Fort Wood).
GRAND TERRE ISLAND	Undetermined amount in gold and jewels belonging to retired pirate from Laffite's fleet.
MARSH ISLAND	Undetermined amount in gold doubloons.
TIMBALIERS ISLAND	Undetermined amount in gold doubloons.
RED RIVER BEND	Confederate gold. Beware!....reportedly there is a ghost of a Confederate soldier guarding it!
LAKE CHARLES	A cauldron of gold and silver in lowlands south of city.
ABBEVILLE	Confederate gold.
ON LOUISIANA COAST	Sterling silver horse six foot tall in a sunken Spanish galleon.

J DeHart

Creole Boatbuilders

The first Louisiana highways
were bayous, rivers and lakes,
Traveled by steamboat, tug or barge
or whatever a man could make.

The flat boat, skiff or pirogue
was common along the way,
For work or only for pleasure
'twas used throughout each day.

Shrimp boats were always best
with designs second to none,
When built by local Creoles
in teams of father and son.

They've always met each challenge
with skills like no other,
To provide that needed craft
be it tugboat or a trawler.

So lift your hats to the king of craftsmen
down bayou country way,
May God bless and let them reign
forever and a day.

Old Cane River

We need not search through the pages of history to find the gentle hearts and peaceful atmospheres of a long time ago. Those elements of pleasant environments exist today in the beautiful Cane River country below the historic town of Natchitoches. Begin at the little village of Cloutierville where there is much legend and folklore and many treasures of Cane River plantation life. Here we dwell in the shadows of a rich heritage that is so unique to Louisiana. This rambling French village was named for Alexis Cloutier, a wealthy planter who built the mansion that became the home of authoress Kate Chopin.... it is now a very worthy museum.

To travel fifteen land miles to Natchitoches one must journey thirty or more winding water miles on this beautiful crystal river-lake in an unhurried fashion in order to appreciate those interesting and rich flavors of Cane River country; a land of old plantations, a land known as "Le Cote Joyeuse" (the Joyous Coast). So pleased was this stream with the "Eden" it had created it just wandered leisurely back and forth to extend its stay in this pleasant land.

So, journey into this country of "gens de couleur" (people of color) where there are men of stature with handsome features and cream-skinned girls with beautiful gentle eyes. These are French people who are zestfully flavored with tinges of African, Spanish and Indian; skilled artisians, cuisiniers, shoemakers, woodworkers and farmers, all serving the needs of the other. These are the people of Isle Brevelle where generation after generation have known only the Catholic faith. This is rural France with shades of mulatto, it is the land of the Metoyers, the Roques, the Slives and others of a special caste set aside from the rest of the world in a chosen land. Here today there is that same calm and peace of a century and one-half ago; only in Louisiana could a people of such unique culture exist.

On these tranquil shores we find the plantation where Isle Brevelle's "Big Father" Augustin Metoyer built his home and called it "Yucca"....it is now known as Melrose. This interesting relic alone represents a whole segment of Louisiana history; it was a factory of culture where talented artists and writers lived together, researched together, wrote best sellers and painted masterpieces. Ghosts of many of the greats still roam the rooms, gardens and riverbanks; writers Erskine Caldwell, William Spratlin, François Mignon, Lyle Saxon, Ada Jack Carver and to join them for an occasional cordial is Kate Chopin of "Bayou Folk" fame. Artists Sudyan and Degot work side by side in the "Yucca" studio. Just across the river on the west bank is St. Augustine's Roman Catholic Church, a gift to the people of Isle Brevelle from Augustin Metoyer. To the rear of the church are tall tombs of the cemetery bearing many names of founding families.

Once again we are upon the peaceful river basking in the treasures of this pleasant land. Flowers are everywhere; colorful lotus, green hyacinth explode into lavender blooms, wild irises and pansies embellish the shores. It is sweet and lazy along the Cane, bordered by willows, oaks, cypress, cattails and redberried trees while hundreds of birds fill this scented air with song; buntings, waterthrust, orioles and a multitude more.

There are numerous reflections of the past that bring to mind the days of old when tranquility reigned and where the joys of peace were surpassed only by the charming manners and friendliness of the natives. Here the mulattoes warmly embrace the land that they cherish so much and want others to love it as they do. Time seems to be of no essence, not many places can a person's mind be as much at ease as on this Joyous Coast of Isle Brevelle.

The sweet smell of freshly ground corn tells us of neighboring plantations where ancient dwellings line the banks, surrounded by massive oaks and cedars. Blooming crepe myrtles and camelias border walkways and cherokee roses entwine themselves unto split rail cypress fences. Overhanging flowering dogwoods drop perfumed blossoms upon the silvery stream. There are endless fields of cotton that were once mixed with tobacco, and in the fall delicious aromas from bubbling kettles of sugar cane syrup cover the countryside. There is an occasional gin with presses that make ready huge cotton cargoes for far off textile mills. Cabins of "bouisillage" lay at a distance from the old steamboat landings and the melodious voices of negroes can be heard in spiritual folk song.

We sense the presence of the spirits of the Prudhommes, the Sompayracs, the Hertzogs, the Murphys, the Roubieus and other noble people; souls that linger on in their heavenly gardens and maintain enriched inspirations of the yesteryears. They were the builders of the plantation homes that are now so well preserved as tributes to those pioneering fathers of this beautiful Cane River country; a land that has become such a relished favorite; a land where gentle faces and kind hearts are the custom rather than the exception.

This pleasant journey becomes further enriched by the charming little town of Natchitoches which lies at the northern reaches of the Cane River. It is a very precious gem and is to Louisiana what the pit is to the peach; located in the core of the state, its rich heritage reaches out in all directions. This jewel has maintained all the magic of the days of yore, it has treasures that forever reflect the wonderful old time Creole spirit of Louisiana. It is not a town that quietly sleeps, it is a town that can sleep in quiet. Natchitoches is intensely appealing and should be a shrine dedicated to peace. It renders to its people enchanting values that can be found only in this land of the "Cane River of Old Louisiana."

MELANIE

Gems From Coastal Waters

All hands are busy for the coming of the spring season. Nets must be mended, hulls to be caulked, broken rigging spliced and the rotted and worn is repaired or replaced; all will be made like new. This, the trawler is their subsistence and will be their home on outlying waters for months to come.

Yes, all must be made ready as springtime approaches; ready for the "big day" when the multitudes will celebrate its coming in holy recognition of God's presence among them.

The altar is covered in white and decorated with colorful wild flowers while moss draped oaks form a living cathedral on the bayou shores. Rays of sunlight reach through to the water below and glisten like crystals between lavenders and greens of the hyacinth. Incenses enrich the breezes sending out consecrated scents to the worshipers. Thousands on shore and in the boats join together in prayer when the bell rings out to begin the mass for the *"Blessing of the Fleet."*

Together, they ask God's guidance and for an abundance within their trawls, and they ask Him to bring them safely home from the perils of the open sea. They ask of Him to spare them and their loved ones from tragedy and they thank Him for the many blessings bestowed upon them in previous seasons.

Scoured and sparkling with fresh paint and with colored banners flying high in the breezes the shrimp boats line the water's edge to pass in review as the Bishop sanctifies each with holy water. Earlier in his sermon he had compared these seamen of the day to fishermen of nearly two thousand years before them, they who had become disciples of Christ. And for a time there are solemn thoughts and prayers, remembering the past while thinking of the future.

Then....from this revered mood in prayer the scene changes into festive gaiety with jovial songs and dancing! Tables are covered with huge buckets of early seafood taken from steaming sugarhouse kettles that are filled with spiced and flavored waters.... feastly reminders of the many months to come. There are little girls in fresh new taffeta dresses, mama with a new bonnet and papa in his Sunday khakis. There is music with the accordian and the fiddle and young men flirt with pretty girls. There is strengthening of old friendships and the making of new ones. And, there are more delightful songs, dancing and feasting before all will settle down to a long season of work with no play.

* * * * * * * * *

Papa and the boys are up long before the dawn's first light strikes the top of the mast. All must be checked again; supplies of food and repairs and various medicines. At sea each one must become many; a boatman, a fisherman, handy-man, skilled repairman, a cook and perhaps even a doctor. The tenderfoot must learn quickly and without choice.

As many as fifteen boats may makeup a party with several parties to the fleet. At the break of dawn the lead boat signals with blasts of the whistle and one behind the other they take their position; shrimp boats are on their way, women and children with saddened faces crowd the water's edge to wave farewells to their men. They will not return for weeks and perhaps then only to replenish supplies and once again return to the sea. Throughout each day only the company boat returns home with the rich catches from the fleet.

Filled nets bear many pounds of jumbo shrimp with an abundance of other sea life; scurrying crabs, squid, sea horses, flounders, catfish and hundreds of others, and surely there is plenty of seaweed.

Except for what will be used for the crew's meal, all but the shrimp must return to the waters. Shrieking gulls constantly encircle the boats for these delightful throw backs, giving to them effortless feasts as no other winged life has ever enjoyed. These are the freeloaders of the shrimpers fleet.

Occasionally a net is removed from the waters bearing large gaping holes with the loss of a catch. A porpoise has taken a hearty bite from the treasures within. Bitterness is stimulated once again toward that seafaring monster who has been a long time enemy to all fishermen.

Young Vic down the way a few hundred yards on the boat to the south (first time out with his papa and brothers) has fallen from the spar breaking his arm. Jacque swims over to help, he has splinted broken arms before. Vic's brother, Alton, goes home with him on the "company" boat. Alton joins the others on the return trip, but Vic will miss much of his first season with that healing arm. Surely, next time he will take a firmer grip.

On the Gulf waters where violent weathers are frequent there are many mishaps and sometimes tragedy, bringing grief to the entire fleet and their families. Though it may come to only one, the disaster is suffered by all; they have lived together, they have worked together and they have prayed together for such a long time each feels every sorrow of the other. Togetherness in family and togetherness in friendships is a way of life in the bayou country.

To pass the time of long idle hours after supper, night after night many play poker or bourrè by lantern light. Others may sing songs of home or they may think pleasant thoughts of Phelia, Regina, Felicité or Renée who is waiting at home for them, while off in the distance can be heard the lonely melodious sounds from Valcour's harmonica.

Nights are long, but the presence of each other and excitements of the working day can shorten those heartfelt weeks away, longing for friends and loved ones.

At the season's end the take is rewarding and there will be other trips soon to look forward to, bringing aquatic treasures that will overflow the dinner plates of America, both in the home and in fine restaurants afar. Fleets of Barataria, Vermilion and Lafourche from the Sabine to Delacroix and along bayous of Terrebonne will all venture out once again seeking those jewels beneath Louisiana waters; translucent gems that will furnish livelihoods and delicious dishes to thousands for many years to come.

FRENCH CULTURES OF LOUISIANA

French Creoles

In the late 1600's French explorers were sent by King Louis XIV to France to carve a new territory from a wilderness on the North American continent. Trading villages and outposts were established, forts constructed and soldiers assigned.

Next came gentlemen planters from the countrysides of Alsace-Lorraine and other farm land regions of France. Later, there were dignitaries sent from the courts of King Louis XVI and aristocrats with noble titles. Political exiles loyal to the crown during Napoleonic Wars were followed by ranking officers and honored soldiers from Napoleon's own armies. The new pioneers brought with them their wives and their children to settle this new region owned by France. Those were the fathers of the original "Louisiana Territory."

Their children married offsprings of other noble French settlers, although many of the sons sought wives from the ranks of the famed "Les Filles á la Cassettes" (The Casket Girls). This select group were wellbred orphaned girls of France who were sent to New Orleans by the king to be properly tutored by the Ursuline Nuns for the sole purpose of becoming wives of sons of upper class French families of Louisiana. (See "Ursuline Nuns" in Spiritual Cameo's chapter). Children from above mentioned unions formed the "tap roots" of the Creole society of Louisiana.

This was the origin of a caste that was to fashion moral standards and social behaviors for a society that became the predominent culture of Louisiana for many many generations thereafter. All descendants of that caste are known as French Creoles of Louisiana. It is a society set aside by their heritage, a product of the pure blood European French of the refined class.... an aesthetic well-knit race extremely proud of their French inheritance.

Creole men were well educated, reared in the best schools available, many attending the finest institutions of Paris. Most of them spoke English as well as French very fluently. They were men of honor who became planters, merchants, importers, politicans, lawyers, doctors, bankers and brokers. Those of the middle class became bookkeepers, scribes, cashiers, clerks and shopkeepers. They were the foremost gentlemen who never appeared in public without a coat and cravat. They were men who formed a government that fashioned a new and civilized world from a primitive wilderness. They were the men who established a free enterprise that became the true foundation of Louisiana's prosperity.... long before "Les Americains" arrived to reap the harvest of their labors.

Although "the Americans" never did credit the French with having such attributes, Creole men were excellent business managers who accepted the problems, weighed the accounts and made careful analysis before coming to a decision and that decision was rarely ever changed. They had to be sound in their business judgements or not many of them would have achieved the wealth that so many obtained. They built empires with their heads rather than with their hands and back.

They were men whose families were the paramount reason for life. The Creole father was the absolute head of the household.... his word was final in all matters. Yet, he was loving, generous to a fault, compassionate and if it ever became necessary he would spend all he owned for the sake of his children's well-being.

Creole men usually placed women on high pedestals of adoration. However, some marriages were "mariage de convenance," (marriage of convenience), where the union of a boy and girl of two prominent families was contrived by their parents in order to unite those two Creole families. Since those marriages were not a product of love it often resulted in the husband seeking out a concubine "wife." (See "Les Quadroon Concubines" under A Blend of Old New Orleans Flavors). Yet, in spite of this lack of love in some marriages the Creole man was forever ready to defend the honor of his wife and children, even if it meant a duel unto death, which was very much a segment of Creole society. Perhaps one of the greatest faults of Creole men was their mania for gambling, they had an extreme passion for it, especially at the card tables where fortunes were lost and won overnight.

The Creole woman was a devoutely religious person (Roman Catholic), a devoted wife and mother, an excellent housekeeper - economical and extremely hospitable. The "Americans" often described the average Creole woman as "Vivacious with attractive features and immaculate complexions, lively expressive eyes, extremely beautiful long hair and exceedingly tasteful in dress.... and always very soft spoken." The only make-up a woman wore was crushed rose petals for her cheeks and she would never leave the privacy of the home unless in full attire.... gloves and all.

Many of the Creole homes had a "mammy." This was a negress nurse who took care of the children and throughout her life shared their affections along with the parents. Never considered to be in the ranks of a servant, she occupied a position in the household that equalled a member of the family. She cared for the children, disciplined them and loved them as though they were her own. She traveled with the family everywhere; shopping, picnics, visiting friends and even when the family vacationed in Europe. After growing old she was retired and supported by the family to the end of her days. "Mammies" were very special people in the Creole household.

Creole children were usually well educated at the finest schools available. When young, they were tutored by private teachers at home and after becoming of age boys were boarded at schools in New Orleans, Jefferson College at Covnent, St. Charles College at Grand Coteau and many were even sent to Paris. Girls received their education with Catholic nuns at St. Michaels at Convent, Ursuline Convent in New Orleans, St. Basils Academy at Plaquemine, Mount Carmel at New Iberia, Sacred Heart Academy at Grand Coteau and some also went to Paris, living with relatives until their education was completed.

Young men were trained for the sole purpose of taking over the family business and often the father moved aside to make room for the sons. Girls were trained to become wives and mothers, to raise families, but her schooling wasn't limited to domestic training alone. Besides housekeeping, sewing and cooking, she was schooled in economics, reading, writing, arithmetic, geography, English, music, dancing, painting and the all important art of hospitality.

Young couples were never allowed to be alone, courting was always done with a chaperone present. The virtues of a young girl was well guarded, courtship to marriage was done in formal fashion.

Weddings were always arranged by the parents and were very elaborate with a feast highlighting the event. The father put up a dowery for his daughter which usually consisted of a considerable amount in either money or property and sometimes both.

Honeymoons were observed with absolute respect. The bride and groom could not leave their room for at least five days. Meals were brought in to them by special servants who were assigned to their every needs. After the wedding the bride could not be seen on the street for at least two weeks. If "honeymooning" at the boy's home the girl could not even visit her own parents during that period. Those customs were practiced in respect for the privacy of the couple and for the sacredness of their wedding.

Creoles are a gay and festive people who love to entertain and to be entertained, they will create a condition or a situation just to have something to celebrate. Early Creole entertainments more often than not included all members of the family. There were grand balls, elegant house parties, musical recitals, plays and church socials with a variety of events were frequent. They were very fond of the theatre; drama and comedy equally enjoyed, but, perhaps their most favored pleasure was the opera. It was a strong fiber in the fabric of their culture. Opera was attended with great enthusiasm and future events were always planned with eagerness. It was also the source of "coming-out" for young Creole girls.... her first formal contact with social circles was at the opera. She was presented to the Creole society much in the same fashion that debutants are introduced into the American society. New Orleans was the culture center for the entire South and the French Opera House was its headquarters; it was a great temple dedicated to the art.

Creoles still love to entertain at home, often with lavish parties and dinners, dining rooms are usually the center of activity. Large oval tables covered with damask cloths are dressed with china, silver and crystal and embelished with numerous varieties of meats, vegetables, breads, sauces, cakes, custards, pies, fruits and wines. Creole foods are prepared and presented in excellent fashion and savored with great delight. Sunday dinners (served at mid-day) are elaborate with dozens of family members attending, it is a very joyous occasion. (See "Creole Cooking" under French and Acadian Cuisines).

The Creole lifestyle is based primarily around family and religion, it is of great spiritual and social importance, their religion is of the Catholic faith. They have an intense love for their church; religious events and feasts are looked forward to with great interest. The Creole woman, being very sincere and devoute, is the religious core of the family. Every early bedroom had an altar, even if only simple, and always there was a candle to burn. These were usually miniature shrines to Christ and the Virgin Mary. Women have always been very much attached to their prayer book and rosary and attend church services with deep veneration.

To the early Creole family Christmas was strictly a religious holiday honoring Christ. "La Messe de Minuit" (Midnight Mass) was particularily special, services being magnificently soul-reaching; church and altar decorated beyond description. Christmas Day was spent very quietly at home with members of the immediate family. What Christmas Day has become to modern time, New Year's Day meant even more to the early Creoles. There were visits to many various homes, exchanging gifts, giving toys and presents to children and joyful season greetings were always in order of the celebration. Throughout the day the home was generously garnished with delicious treats; candies, fruit, cakes, pies and an abundance of wines, cordials and liqueurs. (Whiskey is rarely ever served in the Creole homes). Finally, the day was ended with a sumptuous family dinner. The principle drink for greeting the New Year was eggnog which was generously spiked with the finest brandy.... New Year's Day was one of the most merrily celebrated of all holidays.

Louisiana's French were responsible for some of the most unique and practical styles of architecture ever developed in North America. The Creoles created designs that are still very functional today. Not only are they attractive in appearance but they are also very practical in Louisiana's climate. The Louisiana Colonial house, the Creole cottage and the loveable little "shotgun" cottage are just three of the many architectural expressions of French Louisiana. They exhibit a great love for broad galleries and large spacious rooms with tall windows and doors. Their homes reflect warm pleasant atmospheres.... a projection of the character of the people housed within.

* * * * * * * *

Facets of Creole lifestyles, personalities, customs and special religious practices are so numerous it would take an entire book on the subject to properly portray a complete picture of the true Creole society.

Areas where the roots of that culture ran deeper and are still well established are in New Orleans, all along the Mississippi River to Pointe Coupee Parish and in the Avoyelles, Attakapas, Teche and Cane River regions.

Blue blood Creole names that have graced the registers of Louisiana social, business and political life are many; such popular names as Prud'homme, de la Houssaye, Duchamp, Bienvenue, Boutté, Fortier, Dupre, André, Durand, d'Estréhan, Guillot, Labiche, Patout, Trahan, LaSalle and Fuselier are just a few of the many family names which are of Creole stock. They have always displayed a quality of natural inborn refinement that makes them stand out as special people in Louisiana's history. They fashioned the aesthetic patterns for a social and spiritual environment that has lasted into modern times; many Creoles of today still preserve their beloved heritage with a sacred indulgence. Although the Creole society may never again return as the dominant culture it once was it has made profound impressions upon the everyday life structure of Louisiana that will remain forever.

To the Creoles, Louisiana owes an enormous debt; the spectacular Mardi Gras, exquisite world famous cuisines, a fascinating medley of architecture and picturesque cemeteries ("Cities of the Dead"), unique religious practices, fantastic amounts of splendor and gaiety, and a delightful array of unusual customs with unparalleled portions of charm, dignity and superb hospitality.

EARLY ACADIAN FARM

Early Acadians

Acadians are direct descendants of the French peasants who were expelled from Nova Scotia by the British in 1755, and who came to settle in Louisiana. Much has been printed about their banishment from their country, of their plights and of their ventures that led thousands to settle on the rich soils of southern Louisiana. But, very little has been written telling of their everyday lifestyles and customs during the early years after establishing their homes in the wilds along the bayous and on the isolated prairies of their newly found land.

Although many of the Acadians who first came to Louisiana became trappers and fishermen, most of them, after receiving Spanish grants of small parcels of land, went into farming. Their trials and hardships were many and with very little more than strong wills and bodies they cleared the land, built their homes, made vegetable gardens and hunted the wild for their food. Little by little they acquired enough equipment and livestock to turn this fertile frontier wilderness into civilized and productive farming hamlets, which today covers large portions of the Attakapas, Teche and Lafourche countrysides.

On a much smaller scale, the Acadian farms were similiar to the larger plantations in the sense that they were self-sustaining. Crops of corn, rice, vegetables, fruit, nuts and wildlife not only furnished food for them, but also for their livestock. With cotton and wool raised on the farm they made fabric for clothing; techniques for spinning and weaving were brought with them and were handed down to many generations afterwards. Cured Spanish moss or feathers made good stuffing for pillows and mattresses. Shoes were made from animal hides and fur gave them warm winter clothing. Even buttons were carved from wood or made from fruit pits. Nearby forests furnished an abundance of wood for lumber to construct buildings and fuel for cooking and heating. Those families fortunate enough to have several adults made quicker progress towards development. Every member of the family, from young children to the elderly, contributed their fair share with mature and responsible attitudes.

Domestic farm animals were acquired by bartering with corn, cotton and vegetable products from the farm, even cooking utinsels and farming tools were obtained in this manner. The "marchand charette" (traveling stores), an old tradition from provincial French farming areas, also served as mobile gazette to give them news about the outer world. At first large implements such as wagons and plows were homemade, but these were later replaced with sturdier and more efficient equipment by acquiring them through the bartering method.

Construction of the early Acadian home was unique and distinct in design. The roof had a very high peak with a gable at each end. The front gallery ran full width of the house and was recessed underneath the main roof to become known as a "interieur galerie" (inside gallery). A stairway led from the gallery into the "grenier" or attic which was used as a "garconniere" for the young boys to sleep or as a loom room for spinning and weaving. Additions to the house were frequently done by adding another house of identical design and size alongside the old one, gable to gable; or perhaps a dining room and kitchen was built to extend out from one side.

Another distinctive feature of the Acadian home was the "tablette," or shelf built to extend outside the kitchen window forming a table to wash dishes, for cutting vegetables or to do other kitchen chores while keeping company with someone working outside. It was also easy to keep an eye on chickens and livestock while the "bonne femme" (good woman) did her kitchen work.... farm animals were always endangered by predators from the nearby wilderness. The "tablette" also served as a convenient place to quickly cool freshly baked custards, pies and cakes.

Yards and pastures were always fenced with different styles in fencing, the "paling" type with vertical boards placed close together protected flower and vegetable gardens in the immediate vicinity of the home from all animal invaders. In the very early days "stockade" type fences with posts driven in the ground side by side were used for this purpose. More economical "pieu" or post and rail fences kept larger farm animals within safe confines of the property and away from the dangerous elements of the swamps and forests.

A circular watering pond for livestock and fowl known as a "dig" was essential on every farm. This was created when removing clay to make insulation for the "bousillage" walls of the home and for constructing mud chimneys. Louisiana rains kept this dish-shaped hole constantly filled with water for cooling the animals. Hogs were never allowed to enter a "dig," in a very short time the water would become unsuitable for the other animals, so the hogs were kept in other fenced-in areas with a separate water supply. All family cooking, drinking and washing water was obtained from covered rainwater cisterns and barrels. Eventually wells were dug, but the cistern was used for clearer and less contaminated cooking and drinking water. Even then, water for human consumption was usually boiled before using.

The Acadians of south Louisiana were happy people with strong family ties, they have diligently preserved their customs, traditions and religious practices (devoute Catholics) with a great degree of loyalty. The "bonne femme" of the family played a most important role; she and the daughters made fabrics, sewed clothing, worked in the home, gardens and attended the livestock. Whenever necessary she often worked alongside her husband and sons in the fields. The women always had flowers growing in the yard; fragrances of roses, marigolds, cannas and others forever scented the air, and without fail, there was the favorite Cape Jasmine bush. Their vegetable gardens were the most complete and as beautiful as could be found anywhere.

Love was a very important element in the making of happy marriages which were usually very successful and productive; it was not uncommon for a couple to have a dozen children. There was always discipline supreme within the household and there has always been a very generous display of mutual respect between the young and their elders.

Cajun weddings were very special events that included the entire community. It took on atmospheres of a festival, beginning in the morning with the wedding mass, communion and the church wedding, after which came a feast of Cajun foods ending with a Cajun dance that lasted well into the evening. Acadian bands furnished the music for the entire event.

They were fun loving people and very innovative with their entertainments which usually included the entire family. Being fond of music and dancing their "Saturday Night Fais Dodo" was a very important event. In the early years these took place in one of the homes where everyone from the neighboring farms would gather for music and dancing. Musicians were members of the communities skilled in playing the fiddle, accordian and the triangle, or "ting-a-ling" as they called it; the guitar was later added. Since the event usually lasted throughout the night, little children were all put to sleep in one room, thus the name "Fais Dodo," an Acadian expression which means "go to sleep little one." But, regardless of how long into the night it did last or how tired they were when it ended, everyone devoutly attended Sunday morning religious services.

The Acadians had a passion for community gatherings and during the early days there were many mattress making and quilting parties. Canning and preserving events were extra special because the children could also participate. Men had a special appetite for gambling, even if only for small stakes. They loved to play cards, their favorite games being poker and bourre. Horse racing on two horse straight-away-quarter mile tracks has always been a favorite among them. Cockfights were considered special gambling entertainment for men. Gamecocks were well cared for and were given specialized training just as prizefighters would receive. Special arenas were built for the events which were often. This sport was not considered inhumane since roosters were well trained to protect themselves before they were ever exposed to a contender, just as a human boxer would be professionally trained before entering the ring.

Perhaps the most important of all Acadian gatherings was the "boucherie," an event looked forward to with enthusiasm during the entire spring and summer by all members of the family. As soon as the air began to chill in the autumn months the "boucherie" (a cooperative butchery) was announced. At a previously selected homestead several families would gather before sunrise. Off in a distance, away from the women and children the men would butcher prize hogs, then the entire group would work together throughout the day cutting roasts, chops, salting and smoking hams, making sausages, boudins, cracklings, pickling hog feet and making headcheese. Before returning to their home in the evening each family received their proportionate share of meat. When this supply was depleted another boucherie was called, but at a different farm and they then furnished the hogs. This system of rotation lasted until the spring months. Pork was always a favorite meat for the Acadians, but supplements as well as substitutions in the hot months were made with domesticated and wild fowl and animals.

Their tables seemed to be forever covered with food. All were excellent cooks and very proficient when it came to creating new dishes from leftover foods. Nothing was ever wasted. The Acadians were credited with creating many of the delicious Louisiana style dishes that have become so popular over the years; jambalaya of all kinds, chaudin, grattons, boudin, andouilles and other sausages, many crawfish dishes, to name only a very few of their delicious foods.

The patois of French spoken by the Louisiana Acadians is of less pure French and is even different from that of the Acadians of Nova Scotia. For many generations both cultures had been completely separated from their native France and when new conditions, subjects and words were presented to them it became necessary to create their own particular phrases, expressions and word variations to suit the needs of communication. And too, because of the different nationalities which in time were absorbed into Louisiana's French society, German, Spanish and Negro expressions or slangs soon became a common part of the Acadian French language. Their dialects, expressions and mannerisms varied considerably even within their own neighboring settlements. Most Acadians, when speaking, use many slang words and substitutes in their French speech.... Creoles would never think of doing this.

Family customs, cultural traditions, lifestyle and religious beliefs of the Louisiana Acadians were very unique and even their food was always very individualistic. For over two hundred years they have left indelible impressions of a distinct and special culture in Louisiana and America.

FAIS DO-DO

CAJUN ROUNDUP

Creole & Acadian Cuisine

The differences between these two elements of French society in Louisiana must first be understood before their different styles of cooking can be readily separated. (See Creoles of Louisiana and Early Louisiana Acadians this chapter). The Techeland offers an ideal transition from French Creole to Acadian cuisines, in this area more than any other part of Louisiana the two cultures are better compared. Here in the Techeland French Creoles and Acadians have lived side by side for over two hundred years, yet each has maintained its own separate characteristics of living and cooking.

CREOLE COOKING

Servants in early French households were highly trained slaves and the "Cuisiniere" (cook) was an excellent culinary artiste. She mastered cooking with great pride, making every dish an artistic achievement. Her position in the household was highly respected.

Often when preferred herbs, spices or foods were in shortage the cuisiniere sought other methods to please the taste buds by concocting exciting new dishes from older French recipes. Many of those culinary inventions were created with foods, herbs and spices from African, Spanish or Louisiana Indian practices and preparations. Those dishes were so well received at the early dining tables that they became standard on menus for Louisiana cooking; creations that became some of the most unique and tastiest dishes in all the world. This is what became known as the French Creole Cuisine of Louisiana.

Although the Creole dishes are always made with the highest quality of ingredients and prepared with the best culinary skills, patience is perhaps one of the most important factors; patience while preparing and patience while cooking. And, always there is the "cast iron pot and skillet" for uniform heat. There are no quick-cook methods when preparing Louisiana Creole foods; slow cooking and blending of sauces is absolutely necessary to achieve the proper tenderness and unique flavors. Natural food additives are used only to enhance the natural tastes but never to the extent of masking those true flavors of meats and vegetables. Artificial seasonings and synthetic tenderizers are forbidden in the French Creole kitchen.

Each dish is cooked separately and is served separately, often with an assortment of preparations. The Sunday dinner table of the early Creole family often had over half a dozen different meat dishes, as many various kinds of vegetables and a variety of breads and desserts. Assorted fine flavored wines were always served and fresh fruits and nuts directly from the orchards were abundantly dispersed around living and dining areas. Coffee of unusual flavors and aromas was a must and always kept warm throughout the day.

The "roux" (a special mixture of cooking fat, flour and seasonings) is very essential to prepare many of the meats and gumbos, it is a must in the rituals of Louisiana French cooking; a must in order to achieve the fine rich flavors of the many delicious dishes.

The French Creole cook's talent to blend sauces and gravies along with other special culinary skills are matched by no other. Foods are individually served so that each may be savored for its own distinctive merits in flavor and bouquet. Planning, cooking, serving and eating a meal in the French Creole home is a treasured ritual, one of much importance to their everyday lifestyle. Dining in their homes often takes on the appearance of an aristocratic banquet, especially when guests are being entertained. With the French Creole, a meal can become a major entertainment and on leisure days breakfast often lasted until dinner and dinner extended into supper time.

The taste of Creole foods prepared by private cooks in homes are usually far superior to those cooked in restaurants because of the extra time made available to the cuisiniere and the elegant manner in which it is served.

The best French Creole foods have always been in areas around New Orleans and in Bayou Teche country where French influence is so well pronounced.

ACADIAN COOKING

Entire meals for an Acadian family are often cooked in one large pot (again, as with the Creole, always a cast iron pot). Stews, soups, hashes and jambalayas were usual diets of the early Acadian settlers. They later adopted some of the Creole methods and dishes; various gumbos, mirliton, squash, potato and okra dishes and, of course, red beans and rice. Acadian meals were prepared to economically furnish proper nourishment and substance for hard workers, which usually included all members of the family.

Diets for marsh and swamp Acadians consisted mainly of seafoods, wild animals and wild fowl. The farm Acadians used a considerable amount of corn, beans, rice and other staples that could be easily stored for long periods. Homemade dairy products were common; cream cheese, butter, cheeses, etc.

"Boucheries" among the Acadians became very popular, which accounts for their numerous different pork dishes. During the winter months, (when pork did not spoil as easily) friends and neighbors frequently got together to butcher hogs, which was done in festive atmospheres. (See "La Fête du Cochon," this chapter).

Like the Creoles, the Acadians use many natural herbs and spices but favor more of those which are pungent and peppery with stronger aromas and tastes. Although most Acadian foods differ considerably in taste and appearance they still have as much pride in cooking as the Creoles do and their foods are very healthful even if not as attractive.

As with the Creoles, Acadian foods are far better prepared and are much tastier when cooked in the private home kitchen. Cooking and eating of a meal in the Acadian home is usually a family social adventure.

CONCLUSION

Nature has been very kind to the Louisiana cooking artist, giving so much year 'round in foods. From the beginning the Louisiana natives have not been very tolerant of tasteless and poorly prepared foods. The love for delicacies by the French, pungent seasonings of the Spanish, herbs and roots of the Indians and the culinary skills of the Negro could result in only one absolute product; *the most unique and the tastiest dishes in the world are served on the dining tables of Southern Louisiana.*

J DeHart

La Fête Du Cochon

Eager Cajun countryfolk, relatives and friends, young and old, gathered together before daybreak in festive mood to create delightful pork dishes for the coming winter months. Their day begins early with a breakfast of syrup covered "coush-coush" and large steaming pots of freshly brewed Cajun coffee.

Through early morning haze, pale sunlight stretches long golden streaks across Acadian skies. From a distance wailful sounds of a fiddle can be heard while most of the countryside is still asleep. Autumn's air is crisp and great caldrons of water boil up steam that intermingles with the chilly mist of dawn.

As emotions become spirited, readiness is made in fashions that could rival the greatest sacrificial rituals of the "voodoo." Tables are dressed with skillfully honed butcher knives, the all important fattened *cochon* is prepared, zestful spices and herbs are plentiful, and always, generous amounts of hot mustards and pungent peppers.

Musical tempos from the fiddle, the guitar and the accordian are quickened and happy young feet begin to dance the "galop" to a 2/4 beat. Moods become livelier into the spirits of *grand jour de fête,* celebrations surpass the merriments of the popular *fais-dodo.* Even grand-mere and grand-pere struts about for a waltz or two while little children play happy games in nearby pastures.

Throughout this merry day excited hands are busily sculpturing *andouilles, boudin blanc, jambon, boudin rouge, chaudin and fromage de tête de cochon.* And, too, there is *saucisse boucaner,* and do not forget those hors d'oeuvres of amber-colored *grattons* that are so fragile they melt in the mouth like freshly churned butter.

In the afternoon, fires are once again stoked with hardwood and the faint glow of burning embers suddenly brighten into fiery tongues beneath castiron pots of backbone stew, so delicately rich, tangy and smooth. Delicious pork ribs are generously flavored with those spicy sauces that excite everyone's taste buds.

Late afternoon is the time for that long awaited feast beneath the great oaks. Freshly cooked pork dishes are set out amid loaves of savory French bread, platters of delicious "dirty" rice and jambalaya, crispy fresh salads and sweet yams so tastefully candied in their own skins. There are lots and lots of steaming hot chocolate and café au lait.

And, this splendid banquet is further enhanced with cheery Acadian music; happiness is everywhere, the air is filled with gaiety. Festive moods continue into the night until the warm glows of dying embers ushers in the chill of darkness. And, as each with their own share of *cochon* make their way home they once again bring with them joyous memories of another old fashion *CAJUN BOUCHERIE.*

SYRUP
LE IRON
UP BY
RUP MILL, INC.
LOUISIANA
J. DeHart

"Soppin' Good"

T'was first a horse powered grinder
then steam propelled it became,
And now it's more sophisticated
but results are just the same.

Louisiana sugar cane syrup
rich with calcium and iron,
A delicious food for any table
with no substitute of its kind.

Cooked in an open kettle
from pure sugar cane juices,
Nothing added, nothing extracted
and no limits to its uses.

"Soppin' good" with bread and milk
on French toast it's a treat,
With biscuits, hot cakes or fitters
no better taste you'll seek.

In popcorn balls or pecan pie,
in gingerbread, yams and beans,
No matter how it's fixed
you'll see the faces beam.

It's a product of good French people
prepared for you with pride,
In good old Louisiana fashion
with quality as their guide.

EARLY LOUISIANA RICE MILL

SPIRITUAL CAMEOS

J DeHart

Ursulines Of New Orleans

* *They gave hope where there had been despair.*
* *They sheltered the poor and fed the hungry.*
* *They cared for the sick and wounded.*
* *They turned sorrows into happiness.*
* *They changed hate into love, disbelief into faith.*
* *They protected and strengthened the weak.*
* *They educated the ignorant and refined the crude.*
* *And, they brightened the lives of the multitudes who were ever priviledged to know them.*

* * * * * * * *

The grave need for educators for young girls of New Orleans and Louisiana in the early years prompted Governor Bienville to make an urgent request to the King of France to send teachers (preferably Catholic nuns) to Louisiana for this purpose. Because of the persistent efforts of Reverend Nicholas Ignatius d'Beaubois S.J. of the Jesuit Mission in New Orleans this request was generously fulfilled.

The task was presented to the Ursuline Nuns in France who graciously and eagerly accepted that mission. Not only were they to be teachers for the young girls, but they also accepted the duties of nursing at the King's Hospital in New Orleans and to be guardians for the numerous children who had become orphaned in Louisiana.

On February 22, 1727 nine nuns, a novice and two postulants sailed from l'Orient, France on the ship "La Gironde" bound for New Orleans, arriving on July 23, 1727; five months on a journey that had brought many anxieties, freightening experiences, humor, tenseness, adventure and exhausting but rewarding events. This was thoroughly accounted in the diary-letters written by Sister Marie Magdeleine Hachard de St. Stanislaus, the eighteen year old novice who made the voyage with the Ursulines. History records the letters that she wrote to her father in Rouen, France, giving accounts of their voyage and the first year at the convent in the new colony.

The Ursulines were happily received in New Orleans and they immediately set up their convent to begin educating young women and to nurse the sick at the hospital. They first performed their teaching duties in the Kolly residence, a large home provided by a local family for this particular purpose, but later they moved into a new building constructed specifically for a hospital and convent. The present day historic building on Chartres Street was not built for them until 1748, after their first convent had deteriorated rather rapidly due to poor construction and materials.

The Ursulines served New Orleans and surrounding areas in many capacities. They took in countless orphans of white, negro and indian race, and they taught these children the religion with special religious classes for adults as well. They also operated a free school for day pupils and cared for wayward girls. These nuns established the very first Catholic school in America for the specific purpose of educating young women. The convent in New Orleans became one of the finest sites in the colony, with lush gardens that furnished culinary herbs and medicinal plants for treating illnesses. This was very ably taken care of by Sister Xavier who became the very first woman pharmacist ever to practice in America.

From the very beginning of the colony there had been a serious shortage of young refined women of marrying age for the young sons of prominent business-men and planters of the area. Because of the urgent needs a request was made to France for available young girls of respectable nature, and again a request by the colonies was favorably granted. The nuns had hardly established themselves in their new life when several dozen select young girls of tasteful culture and character from orphanages in France arrived in the city to become future wives of Louisiana bachelors.

These girls had been well educated in French convents and as a gesture of good wishes before leaving, the King had provided each with a trousseau encased in handbags that closely resembled little caskets. After setting eyes on these newcomers with their strange looking little bags, the people of the city quickly dubbed them "Les Filles á la Cassette;" thus they became the famed "Casquette Girls" of New Orleans. These girls were later to become distinguished ancestors of many fine and respected Creoles of present day.

The Ursulines were instrumental in moulding the Creole society that is so pronounced in Louisiana. Their convent became the cradle of culture and learning for hundreds of families on plantations and in city homes. This heritage was handed down through the many generations by mothers who had been foster children and pupils of the Ursulines. All girls educated by these nuns were given the best possible training to prepare them for a future life as honorable wives and mothers. They were taught religion, music, painting, needlework, literature, reading, writing, English, French, geography, arithmetic, history and housework. In addition to this, the orphaned girls were also taught such trades as sewing, cooking and preserving in order to further prepare them to obtain better employment should it become necessary when they became of age to face the world on their own.

In 1763 the first Acadians arrived in Louisiana and were warmly received, not only by the people of the city but especially by the Ursuline Nuns. Those outcast refugees from Nova Scotia were very poor and homeless and many were taken in by the nuns who lodged them at the convent until proper arrangements could be made for them to provide a living for themselves. They were later located in other areas of Louisiana (see "Early Louisiana Acadians" under French Cultures of Louisiana).

During the wars of the area the Ursulines treated the wounded from both sides, Confederate or Union, American or British. After the Battle of New Orleans they were cited by the British Crown for their untiring solicitous service to the wounded British of those battles. For many years that followed the nuns were frequently receiving gifts from British and American soldiers alike who had been nursed back to health by these nuns. Such gifts were generous provisions of hams, bacons, fruits and produce.

Every year since 1815 the New Orleans Ursulines have paid homage to Our Lady of Pompt Succor with an annual mass on January 8th. The nuns credit her with having saved the city from falling to the British during the Battle of New Orleans.

The value of the Ursuline Nuns can never ever be adequately appraised, their work in behalf of the needy in New Orleans has been unmeasurably throughout their existence in the city. History has recorded living memories of those beloved nuns who have tirelessly and willingly served mankind with so much kindness and generosity. Those memories will live on forever in the hearts of grateful Americans of all denominations.

Jefferson College

All along the historic old Mississippi River Road between New Orleans and Baton Rouge there are scores of treasures and lasting impressions of the glorious years of a Golden Plantation Era. There are permanent symbols and patterns of life of past generations that represent the dignified customs of many decades ago. On both sides of the river nestled in tranquil shadows of great moss covered trees there remain many memorials to an age when high morals were the custom rather than the exception. And if a genuine peace can be found among people in this modern day, that peace surely would be present on the campus of old Jefferson College. Perhaps it is for this reason that the Jesuit Priests have used it for so many years for the "Spiritual Excercises" of lay Catholic businessmen.

Spacious and superbly manicured green lawns, great magnolias with sweetly scented flowers and majestic anicent oaks create enchanting atmospheres of a revered serenity.

Sprouting from that emerald lawn are twenty-two sparkling white pillars which front a huge monument that has been dedictated to the high principles and morals of a civilized Christian world. This grand parade of elegant and prestigious architecture blends so harmoniously with ancient treasures from nature. Over a century and one-half has now gone by since this grand structure was erected and it still stands today as elegant as it ever was.

It is flanked on one side by the equally historic Louisiana Classic "President's Home" and on the other side by a peaceful little white chapel of Gothic design. The whole creates splendid breathtaking atmospheres that extend invitations for us to turn back to those pages of history that speak proudly of the days when successes were measured by hard work and meritorious values necessary for quality goals that benefited all people.

HISTORY OF JEFFERSON COLLEGE

Located on the east bank of the Mississippi about ten miles south of the Sunshine Bridge and near the town of Convent, Jefferson College stands as a glorious reminder of Louisiana's pioneers in education.

It was founded by a group of French-Louisianians headed by Andre Bienvenue Roman who was governor of the state in 1830. In that group was Valcour Aime, the man who became known as the "Prince of Louisiana Planters," the man who set patterns for all modern day sugar plantations. The college was built for the higher education of the young men of Louisiana plantation country. It was named to honor the beloved Thomas Jefferson, third President of the United States.

Construction began in February 1830 and doors to the college were opened to register students in February 1833. By 1836, besides the main building (which measures three hundred feet long and forty-four feet deep), there were five, two story buildings including the "President's House." The twin porter's lodges that presently flank the entrance gate were also existing at that time. German artisians and plasterers from the German Mississippi River coast were hired for the construction of Jefferson College.

In 1842 a great fire gutted all buildings except the President's Home and the porter's lodges, but the college immediately rose again almost before those ashes were cooled. Because of inadequate funds to operate, the college was forced to close its doors in 1852. But, through the persistent efforts of Professor Louis Dufau of Louisiana College at New Orleans the school was once again opened as an institution of higher learning for young men.

Again in 1859 financial difficulties arose and the land with its school and all supporting facilities were purchased by Valcour Aime. It was at that time he had the little Gothic Chapel built as a memorial to his deceased son and daughter, Gabriel and Felicite.

During the Civil War the buildings were occupied and used as barracks by Federal troops. On May 6, 1864 Union soldiers were withdrawn from the area and Valcour Aime immediately made an Act of Donation transferring all of Jefferson College and its properties to the order of Roman Catholic Marist Fathers of France. They then re-established the college under the name of St. Mary's Jefferson College. The school was operated by two distinct faculties, one of English educators and the other of French educators and functioned under this status until 1910 when the French faculty was discontinued.

On January 9, 1931 the Jesuit Fathers of New Orleans acquired Jefferson College from the Marist Fathers and renamed it "Manresa House," making it a retreat area for lay businessmen under the direction of the Fathers of the Society of Jesus. Father Robert T. Bryant, S.J. was its first director.

"Manresa" is Spanish and is the name of a cave in a hillside in Spain where St. Ignatius of Loyola, founder of the Society of Jesus, made his first retreat. It was St. Ignatius who named these retreats "Spiritual Exercises."

"Manresa House" has served for this same spiritual purpose since February 26, 1931, over fifty continuous years. This is the only such place in the United States where Catholic laymen serve in complete silence throughout an entire retreat period.

Sacred Heart Of Acadiana

In the tranquil French-Acadian land, nestled comfortably in the rolling hills of Attakapas country is a sacred remnant of history that has lingered so very graciously into our own age. In the peaceful little town of Grand Coteau, between Lafayette and Opelousas and in the very center of Acadiana is the Academy of the Sacred Heart, a college for young girls which is the second oldest school of high learning in Louisiana. Of two hundred and twelve Sacred Heart schools around the world this academy is the oldest in continuous operation.

This fine institution of cultural and academic values was founded by the Sisters of the Sacred Heart to educate the daughters of the planters of this Attakapas and Techeland region. In spite of yellow fever epidemics, devastating fires, ravaging floods, famines and disasters of the Civil War it has served in this capacity continuously for one hundred and sixty years.

Mother Eugene Aude, who had been a member of the Napoleonic court of France, and Sister Mary Layton came from St. Louis by boat down the Mississippi, into the bayous, then overland by oxcart and finally on horseback until they reached Grand Coteau. And, on October 5, 1821 with only an eight student enrollment Mother Eugenie and Sister Mary opened the academy in a two story building on land donated by Charles Smith from his plantation. (That structure was destroyed by fire in 1922). In 1830 the present three and one-half story brick building was built and at the same time the school's famous gardens, patterned from the French garden of Bishop Boussuet, was laid out. In time, other buildings were added.

In 1838 St. Charles College, a Jesuit school for young men, was built nearby with bricks donated by the academy. This school was destroyed by fire in 1908, but was immediately rebuilt as it stands today. Other buildings were later added and the present day complex of the two schools and St. Charles Church along with supporting buildings share the serene shades of beautiful pines and oaks situated on one thousand acres of land in northeastern Grand Coteau. The famous avenue of one hundred and forty year old live oaks were planted by the Reverend Nicholas Point, a Jesuit Priest and the very first rector at St. Charles. The son of William T. Sherman, Civil War Union General, is buried in the cemetery. He was a Jesuit Priest at St. Charles.

In 1866 a young postulant at the academy named Mary Wilson became critically ill and her miraculous recovery was attributed to Saint John Berchmans. The entire community had prayed in a novena to him for nine days for her recovery. The infirmary was converted into a chapel that exists today in honor of this miracle. Sister Mary Wilson's grave is in the old academy cemetery nearby.

The Academy of the Sacred Heart is now on the National Register of Historic Places. It is so well deserving of this tribute, for this rich farm area of French and Acadian planters has never received a greater gift than that of these Sacred Heart Nuns. These dedicated teachers have helped to mold the fine characters of so many mothers, wives and daughters of south central Louisiana families.

It was those Jesuit Priests of St. Charles College who played the important role of educating the sons of planters. The present day St. Charles College is now a seminary to educate young men for Jesuit Priesthood. It was changed from an open college to a seminary in 1922 and remains serving in this capacity today.

The little community of Grand Coteau with its rich heritage of dignified culture and refined teachings has served well as a valued cornerstone in the development of Louisiana.

J. DeHart

Breakthrough

Break through the past my son and learn your lessons well;
this will be good for you.
Waste not your tomorrows by pampering yesteryear's
bitterness; this can strike you in defeat.

Listen not to those who will guide you in hate with intent
to unlawful dissent; they are deceiving you,
They only rob you of a meaningful purpose to attain;
and remove the reality of your dreams.

Hostile teachings when you are young lead only to set-
backs and scorn; listen not to these.
Earn you way to that honorable position with dignity;
give no shame to those you love.

Weep not for misfortunes that have bereaved those of
the past; allowing yourself to resent.
But rather, think of what America has for you and be
grateful; compare with your ancestor's land today.

God has given to us this country and it has risen above
them all; with faith, amibition and work.
God has given to each of us a means to learn with a
most worthy purpose; throw it not away to waste.

Should you stumble and fall, act not in disorderly contempt;
to fail is no disgrace.
Not to rise up again and strive ahead with pride;
that my son is the shame.

Bring no disfavor to the memories of your forefathers who
have earned for you the blessings of today.
Do not disrespect their efforts with delaying bickerings;
be forever worthy of their trials.

Break through the past, my son, with honorable tomorrows!

J. DeHart

A Religious Heritage

(Religious Hallmarks of Louisiana's Forefathers)

From the tiniest of chapels to the grandest of cathedrals there were magnificent soulful expressions to the everlasting glory of the Christ the King. Dutiful hommage was paid to him with splendid lasting monuments of love; grandeur measures with spiritual inspirations.

Doors were forever open and all were welcome. A state of malice never existed and troubled minds and hearts always found a comforting peace. There was no hour to regulate worship in God's house.... there were no moments of denial to prayer.

Fascinating stained glass windows, captivating pipe organs, kneeling rails of respect and honor, masterfully carved altars and tabernacles of great esteem for the most precious Eucharist; all was embellished so artfully with flowers scented so sweetly with nature's delicate fragrances.

Multitudes of candles for prayer, grouped at stations, twinkling together like closely knitted families of stars amassed in the heavens.... flickering gesters of respectful reminders of the ancient Christians of the catacombs.

The Holy Mass, beautifully extended in soul-reaching Latin; the universal religious tongue so easily translated into spiritually inspired emotions.... understood by everyone, anywhere. Harmonious hymns of unanimous expressions enhanced by multitudes of richly gifted voices aloft singing glorious tributes to Almighty God.

So dearly treasured, the Holy Mass, expressions of pride were made with dignified dress, quality mannerisms and conducts that were always far above that of civil or social heights.

With silent authority the priest earned profound respect for his honored and worthy position:.... one who could so ably convey the word of God, the word of the Church in noble fashion. He represented all, rich, poor, young, old, the healthy and the ailing. He truly distinguished himself as a worthy disciple of Christ; an able shepherd so privileged by God to be a leader of His people.

Wonderful pieces of art professed honor to those who were special in Christ's earthly life; Mother Mary, Joseph, Apostles John, Peter and others.... figures artistically sculpted by hands of gifted artists. Glorious tributes to the Lord, illustrating beauty, respect and splendid admirations for God's own creations.

The beloved Rosary, a sacred symbol of honor and dedication addressed to the Most Blessed Mother and her beloved Son. This, a sincere expression of fidelity without shame, with great pride.

The ever treasured personal Missal, the book of prayer and devotion for celebrating religious occasions. A book of *life* for the faithful within the Church who practiced religion with unmatched devotion.

Melodious bells announcing boldly and proudly a time for Mass, a time for prayer; tolling out noble invitations to all the faithful throughout the land to join together in soulful declarations.

* * * * * * * *

Our forefathers, those dedicated and faithful pioneers, looked to the Lord for wisdoms, for strength and for courage to overcome the numerous obstacles and heartaches that beset them.

They erected beautiful lasting memorials of grand churches to honor Christ, and they endorsed them respectfully with countless pieces of art treasures. Many of those monuments have survived numerous decades of the destructful forces of nature. Some have become priceless historic landmarks while others have fallen prey to lessor qualities in men and materials.... qualities without spiritual inspirations or lasting substance.

Time did not alter the good principles and morals of our forefathers. Their devotion to God was not styled by synthetic "progresses" with continual irresponsible moral and material modifications in order to appease the faithless with imprudent values.

The eminence of the Church was not achieved through whimsical fads or chaotic experiments. Its strength evolved from determined faiths, self-disciplines and quality behaviors with dignified standards that did not waver under tempting trials of crude and immoral values.

Our ancestors did not surrender to those irresponsible experiments on honorable customs and convictions, giving rise to serious doubt. To discard traditional honor and practices was to abandon the strength and the heritage of the Church to those with counterfeit intentions and detrimental influences; they would never have reduced their religious values to such levels of irreverence. And, if they would have changed religious teachings and practices to conform to other concepts they would have no longer considered themselves faithful to their Church and its teachings.

* * * * * * * *

"To destroy the hallmarks of the faith our forefathers had in the Church is to abandon our religious inheritance. That which has been destroyed can never again be recovered. To erase the memories of those noble expressions of devotion to God is to blaspheme the dedication that our ancestors had toward establishing firm roots of spiritual freedom in a land all of us very proudly refer to as "OUR HOME."

COUNTRYSIDE MEMORIES

THE FAITHFUL CISTERN

An Old-time Cypress Friend

It stood out there beside the house
        locking lonely, while there it sat,
With hooped skirts made of cypress
        and a top like a Chinaman's hat.
Hardly ever did it have a mate
        to stand up together with pride,
If there were two they stood alone
        near the house with each a side.

Beneath were walls of solid brick
        with holes up near the top,
And a heavy wooden door
        with some hinges and a lock.
Now, I suppose you'd want to know
        "What good is this thing?" you ask,
Well, you listen for just a while
        and I'll tell you of its task.

Above, it was filled with water
        from good old Southern rains,
That came from atop the house
        in homemade wooden drains.
It gave the water to launder clothes
        and for the dishes in the sink,
For that Saturday evening bath
        or for a cool refreshing drink.

Now, there was another fruitful purpose
        that it served so very faithful,
A place to store some special foods
        from May to next year's April.
There were vegetables and fruits in jars,
        smoked sausage, fish and hams,
Butter and cheeses of every kind
        and delicious jellies and jams.
There was homemade cider or applejack
        and the best of blackberry wines,
There was apricot brandy and cherry bounce
        and drinks of other kinds.

Continued . . . .

Whenever you were able to find
        a home of any worth,
There were always two or three
        a sprouting from the earth.
Like ever so faithful sentinels
        they stood there with much pride,
To guard your food and water
        that was stored so well inside.
T'was nothing you'd rather have had
        you couldn't begin to think,
What's better than a RAINWATER CISTERN
        for protecting your food and drink?

Now if you travel a country road
        look for one within your sight.
Some may seem forlorn and sad,
        others are proud and stand upright.
But, no matter how it may look to you
        be it weathered or well preserved,
Say "Hello" to an old time friend,
        for a mankind it so well has served.

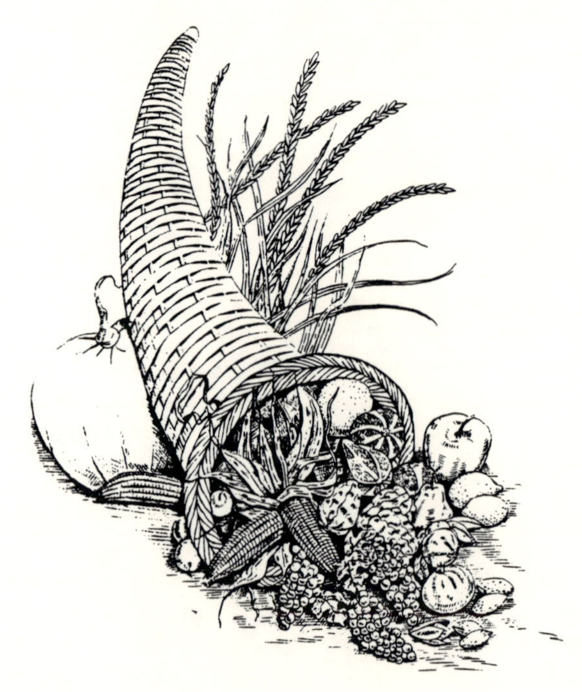

Country Treasures

Walk back into the peaceful shadows of time where scores of humble dwellings surround grand homesteads of noble purpose; where pathways are arched with crepe myrtle and wisteria and where meadows are clothed with daisy, daffodil and butterflies. Flowering sweet clover in the pastures and groves of budding orange trees welcome busy little honey bees.

Dawn is filled with inspiration, ever so beautiful. The golden sun rises in splendor to welcome nature into another glorious day. Pale yellows, pinks and greens filter through a mist of ground fog. A distant church bell tolls and silhouettes of field workers gently bow their heads in solemn angelus; all is quiet with reverence. Then multitudes of birds burst forth into song as if God's own outdoor cathedral had suddenly awaken in choruses of joyous revelry.

Railed fences of hand-hewn unpainted cypress, weathered in beauty by the years, encircle orchards of pear, peach and golden plum. Flowering trumpets of the morning glory open to receive warm rays of sunlight. From a distance come aromas of jasmine and magnolia. Tears of dew drops upon Cherokee roses greet the sunrise with glitter and wild flowers scent the mild breezes with fragrances of iris, buttercup and clover.

Carpets of acorn beneath giant oaks render perpetual feasts for chipmunk and squirrel. Hummingbirds syphon nectar from honeysuckles and Steller Jays pluck purple berries from entwining vines. Horses and cows graze peacefully in yonder pastures of green. All of God's creatures are kissed with the gentle warmth of springtime. Beauties of the countrysides are nature's own and friendships are pure, genuine and plentiful.

Whispering breezes bathe the evenings in freshness while the gay sounds of daytime are toned at nightfall into blissful levels of serenity. Upon shimmering leaves of glossy green, moonbeams dance graceful little minuets to tunes orchestrated by crickets in symphony, while fireflies flicker to mimic the stars in the heavens.... harmonious fantasisms and melodious sounds of nature in glorious concert.

Autumn on the countryside reveals beautiful hues of nature's delightful colors; chestnut browns, oranges and yellows touched with rust while brilliant reds contrast with cool shades of green. Glistening flakes of frost upon the grass in the crisp mornings of an early winter crackle under footsteps of the raven and the robin. Golden eagles, hawks and falcons soar above freshly harvested fields of grain in search of feasting rodents, while redwing blackbirds have a delightful meal in a patch of golden maize left over for their pleasures. Muffled "cooings" and ruffling of feathers in the clumps of wild weeds proclaim peaceful nesting mourning doves.

Nostalgic hearts will forever yearn for those country treasures of the past, when joys of life were simple and good, when pleasures were forever plentiful; things that made the poorest cabin rich and the grandest mansion humble and sensitive to the greatness of God's creations. Those pleasures of the yesteryears were quiet, tender, heartwarming and forever generous; pleasures that were granted only to those who were privileged to know how to appreciate the wonderful gifts of nature and the countless joys extended by their blessings.

OLD IRON HORSE

Old Iron Horse

Our lush land gave to pioneers
abundance of gifts from nature,
Maples, oaks, cypress and gum
for lumber, wood products and paper.

On quicksand and over the swamp
lay miles of steel on trestle,
To reach into the wilderness
where treasures of wood did nestle.

Through distant forest and marsh
over bayou, river and plain,
The old wood burner made its way
with tons of timber by train.

Lonely wails of far off whistles
black clouds of bellowing smoke,
Were signs of "Old Iron Horse"
in an era to compete with the boat.

And, the train men learned new frienships
with reptiles, animals and birds,
And multitudes of strange new life
'came familiar to them in herds.

From these blessings of nature arose
many products of goods to be sold,
The railroad gave a new life
and numerous jobs untold.

The Country Store

There was always a delightful magic
        attached to the *Country Store,*
T'wasn't just a place for buying
        t'was a heck of a lot more.
The storekeeper, who was also postmaster
        and Justice of the Peace,
Sold anything from mailing stamps
        to wagon axle grease.
He was a friend to all of the people
        never turning one away,
The local rural counselor
        who seldom led them astray.

He had anything you'd want to get
        from garden seeds to apparel,
From farming tools to hunting guns
        or pickles right out of a barrel.
High atop from the ceiling rafters
        hung a conglomeration of things,
From horse collars to milking stools
        or fiddles with catgut strings.

Always, there was a barrel of apples
        and bins of cornmeal and rice,
And many different kinds of beans
        or strings of herbs and spice.
Lard was sold on a piece of cardboard
        shaped like a paper boat,
Wooden clothespins and washing boards
        and old fashion laundry soap.

On cold wintry days old timers
        gathered 'round the potbelly stove,
Which was cherry red across the middle
        and filled with chunks of coal.
They played their cards and checkers
        and many a tale was told,
While munching crackers from a barrel
        they pondered the *days of old.*

A great big coffee roaster
        stood handy to make it fresh,
For selling loose in paper bags
        by the pound....*more or less.*
Crockery jars and chinaware,
        cast-iron skillets and pots,
Spoons and forks and kitchen knives
        were sold in assorted lots.

There was one very special section
        that was called *"The Ladies Portion,"*
With buttons, threads, yarn and cloth
        and dozens of other notions.
There were lots of ribbons and laces
        to sew up a fancy dress,
And other kinds of pretty things
        to make her look her best.

It was always lots of pleasure
        thumbing the mail-order book,
A real thrill for any age,
        whether to buy or just to look.
There were pipes for smoking tobacco
        and shaving brushes with mugs,
Sunday shirts and celluloid collars
        with fancy decorating studs.
There were pills to heal the stomach
        and some to make blood pure,
And pills to cure lumbago
        or for any other cure.
There were pretty *"Toilette Sets"*
        and special items to groom,
Hair brushes, mirrors and combs
        and bottles of *"French"* perfume.
Anything you could ever want
        was in that mail-order book,
From riding saddles to buggy whips
        or pots and pans to cook.

The *Country Store* had lots of candy
        some were honey colored toffee,
Others were gumdrops with flavors
        that tasted like rum or coffee.
Caramel popcorn and gingersnaps
        and plenty of candy bars,
Jelly beans and peppermint sticks
        in fancy cut glass jars.

There were so many different items
        on counter, rack or shelf,
To use for work or pleasure
        or perhaps for better health.
T'was always a real good treat
        to go there was no chore,
So when you're on a rural trip
        remember the *COUNTRY STORE.*

River Road Christmas

On the night before Christmas on each side of the river
The pyramids of logs were burning with glitter,
They were stuffed with willows and green bamboo shoots
That were bursting like rockets in a season's salute.

'Waters of the river seemed to glimmer with gold
Bringing spirits of Christmas to the young and the old,
That Old Mississippi was swollen with pride
All ready for Santa to make his Yule ride.

Kids of all ages, both negro and white
Greeted this season with a youthful delight,
The lil 'uns were cuddled all cozy in their beds
While sweet dreams of pralines filled up their heads.

The moon shown so bright on white pillars below
And gleaming church steeples took a lustrous glow,
The sugar mill stack puffed its finale of smoke
Like a toast of good cheer to good countryfolk.

All seemed to stir in anxious poise
When all of a sudden was heard a great noise,
Off in a distance as a thundering band
Came a tiny pirogue and eight happy pel-ican.

The jolly old driver gave a shout and a yell
All knew without a doubt this was Papa Noel,
He was a chubby lil' fellow and a jolly good guy
With a round little belly and a twinkle of the eye.

Quicker than falcons those pelicans came
As he whistled and shouted and called them by name,
"On Philipe, On François, on Gustave and André.
Go Etienne, go Antoine, go Jacques and Honorè."

Old Santa's boat was loaded with toys
For all of those good lil' girls and boys,
To the top of the levee and over the side
On pastures and fields that pirogue did glide,
And with a flip of a wing those birds would swoop
To gallery, to rooftop, to chimney and stoop.

At each of their stops there were bits of delight
To carry them through the cold winter night,
Lots'a pralines, gumbo and coffee with beignets,
Popcorn, eggnog and Bâton Noisettes.
They ate of their fill and drank of good cheer
Then let the good folk know Santa'd been here.

As quick as a rabbit they started to scurry
And rose o'er the levee in a great big hurry,
As they went out of sight over water and land
He gave this salute while waving his hand,
"Merry Christmas good folks old Santa's been here,
Good harvest to y'all and to all a good year!"

Flamme De La Légende Joyeuse

While remembering the Creole forefathers of Louisiana let us return our minds to the days of the French pioneer when happiness was nurtured by love, understanding and great faith in God; when yuletide memories were cherished by riverside planters. And, when hearts were warmed by genuine friendships and neighborly affections.

Address yourself to that era when Louisiana frontiersmen joined together to celebrate the season of joy, the season of love, spiritually enhanced with Midnight Mass. This, a time when the gift of love is so very pronounced.

Above those elevated ribbons of green which border that great river filled with "café au lait," huge bonfires topped with bamboo shoots give forth enormous tongues of crackling fire that leap into the indigo sky like bursting rockets lighting up the heavens. Joyous exaltations dispatch a warm "Saison Accueils" to neighboring farmlands, brightening the way for others to join them in praises of Christ the King.

With excitements generated by the sacred atmospheres of brotherly love they come from every direction with musket on shoulder and prayer book in hand. By pirogue, by skift, by raft, all make their way by the light of the pyramid flames, joining together in happiness their voices in song hail the birth of Jesus; noble gestures in a peaceful winter night wrapped in the warmth of Christmas time.

This Yule time bliss identifies so well with the harvest of sugar cane and this gesture soon becomes a blazing trademark for a successful "Re Colte Saison." The exciting grinding season's end was saluted with pyramids of fire in expression of joy to neighboring plantation folk.

Memories of the "Flamme de Joyeaux" legend did not pass away into the history books; on the contrary, that custom broadened into a very imposing and beautifully romantic Christmas tradition. Lining both sides of the old river from Baton Rouge to Destréhan, scores of bonfires tenderly blaze and hundreds join together for this yuletide event. And, young children are overjoyed that old "Papa Noel" can easily find his way with these glorious fires brightening up a path through a foggy night on the old Mississippi.

This brings to mind visions of a Christmas Eve void of the artificals of tinsel and without the sorrows of the faithless. Under the twinkling stars of the heavens all the faithful join together to praise the coming of our Savior in the delightful atmospheres of flaming pyramids and melodious praise. Today, as it was in the yesteryears, that unique custom of Louisiana Creoles is a magnificent salutation to a very joyous occasion.

BAYOU COUNTRY

What Is A Bayou?

You may ask....*What is a Bayou?*....and since there are so few words that can truly describe the many enchanting qualities that have charmed the multitudes, only vaguely can the delightful magic that overcomes those who travel the bewitching bayou country be portrayed.

* * * * * * * *

A bayou can be a place of mystery and intrigue, a bayou can be a place of thunderous activity, or it can be a place of tranquil beauty. It is not just a waterway, it is not a river, nor is it a lake; it is a placid stream of varied widths with very little motion, a tributary to or from another. Bayous were Louisiana's first highways of travel by multitudes of pirogues, skiffs, rafts and barges; or perhaps a great sternwheeler with massive cargoes, or exciting showboats of pleasure. Pirates have sailed upon them with galleons filled with treasures of silver, silks and gold and battles have been fought across their peaceful shores.

Beneath the stillness of the surface there can be tremendous armies of aquatic life; scores of fishes, reptiles and an abundance of shellfish. Thousands on the wing dwell upon those wealthy shores that are garnished with so much nourishment. Magnificent oaks shrouded with beards of moss spread great protective branches to embrace it in peace. Sparcely topped cypresses create prehistoric atmospheres and like gigantic mirrors countless mysterious beauties are reflected from a motionless surface; great murals of life painted by God's own hand.

Gentle breezes are filled with delightful fragrancies from heavily scented flowers of hyacinth and lilies. Green, purple and red duckweed form colorful patches of pigment like splotches of paint dispersed upon an artist's pallet. An abundance of plant life cover the banks; oaks, magnolias, sweet bay, gum, pecan and many others along with numerous species of aromatic shrubs and vines. Delicate fern of every variety grace massive gnarled roots, and, there is always a wealth of ancient palmettos. This flora and fauna sanctuary is further enriched with an appreciative people of unique societies.

Bayou Lafourche is of peerless appeal, it boasts "the longest main street on earth," a one hundred and twenty mile aqua-highway bordered by numerous vegetable gardens, a rife of floating bridges and countless curious dwellings of an interesting "Cajun" culture. Flowing gently toward the sea, *Lafourche* widens so gracefully with every mile while multitudes of shrimpboats ornament her banks with stately masts and trawling fishnets; shrilling sea gulls soar anxiously above for tidbits of shellfish favors. It is so unique and is so very different from all other bayous.

Without any doubt, the most peaceful, the most romantic and the most fascinating of them all is *Bayou Teche*. Like a beautiful Indian princess of mystery she displays her charms with a gracious dignity that is adorned with treasures found no other place. Her subjects are dwellers of Gallic flavor and of old world magic. Her shores are embellished with numerous antebellum mansions of special distinction. Writers of romantic songs and poetry have portrayed the many blessings of her bewitching folklore. She has allured lovers, enticed adventurers and becharmed romanticists; painters forever endeavor to capture her beauties on colorful canvasses.

Bayous of Louisiana number in the hundreds and criss-cross each other in the fashion of a spider's web. Their names are of exotic nature, from native indian tongue to those from countrysides of France: *Bienvenue, Waukasha, Fordache and Courtableu.... Terre aux Boeufs, Nespique, Choctaw and Parc Perdue.... Choupique, Manchac, Plaquemine and D'Arbonne.... Barataria, Sauvage, Pierre and Terrebonne.* There are bayous through forests, there are bayous through swamps, there are bayous through marshes and there are those that are etched upon farmlands and prairie. Too numerous are they to name them all, but each has its own character striving to outdo the other, to please any interest and to greatly satisfy the many needs of nature in this wonderland of the wild.

A bayou is a refuge, it is a playground, it is an avenue of peace and an expression of happiness. A bayou is a blessing to the wild and to mankind, a marvelous gift from ancient life that has been extended so graciously into our own time.

> *"This enchanting lady, Louisiana, maintains a very magical aura of peace, contentment and everlasting beauty that is enhanced with intriguing mysteries."*

Journey With Me

Come travel with me, my dearest one
        I have a pleasant trip for you,
So close your eyes and picture them now
        those settings you will review.

Let me bring happiness into your heart
        by sharing with you this treasure,
The gift that God has left for us
        to travel in peace with pleasure.

Vision yourself in the Golden Years
        of paddle wheel at the rear,
Sitting with me upon the deck
        with a view that's wonderfully clear.

I take you on this pleasant journey
        both joyous and serene,
Prepare yourself for an exciting voyage
        of bayou country scenes.

As we'll travel look about with care
        for pictures that will last,
And join me in a frequent visit
        with friendships of the past.

We'll begin afloat this shaded stream
        and meander down the way,
Viewing all that it reveals, and listen
        to what it has to say.

When we have reached our journey's end
        there'll be moments we'd like to cherish,
So forever and ever throughout your life
        don't let these memories perish.

THE STERNWHEELER

Tranquil Bayou Voyage

At its beginning the stream is narrow with banks drawing together ever so near, we can almost reach out and touch each one and pluck lilies from the sides. Traveling along we soon see the willows with their drooping branches bending to the water's edge. And as the bayou slowly widens it brings more distance into our view.

Here we will begin those visions to be recalled that will last always in our thoughts with joy. Together we quietly relax and let our minds receive those pictures that will be engraved forever into our hearts, for they will be ours to last a lifetime on earth and throughout eternity.

Soon the quiet waters are encompassed by rich colorful gardens along both banks, scores of tropical flowers are in masses and we look upon them with reverence. They create atmospheres of romantic tranquility.

We are alone, the two of us together in this Eden so beautiful; a paradise anointed with graces from heaven and made sacred by the hand of God. A garden where trees are shrouded with green and great branches reach out in strength, so masterfully and supreme. They are twisted and gnarled and draped with mosses that sway lazily in the breeze, beckoning us unto the shaded shores beneath.

There are hundred of oaks, magnolias and elms that cool the placid water, and numerous flowering shurbs create on stage a magnificently colorful show, while sounds from multitudes of birds bless the air in song.

Gazing upon the waters we see the soft shadows mingle with silvery spots of sunlight, and highlights dance upon the ripples that slowly drifts from sight beneath the paddles of the sternwheel.

Meadows of clover climb gradually away from the banks of the stream. They are garnished with buttercups and flowers of daisy with pleasing aromas, all becoming harnessed by neat unpainted fences of cypress; they too seem to be from the hand of God. Far off into the distance are vast fields of sugar cane that reach to the horizons, and, as though it is a lone sentinel stationed to guard those sheets of swaying green, a giant mill rises up in overpowering dominance.

In awe our breath is taken at the sight of gigantic pillared mansions with wide galleries and stairways that seem to reach up to the sky, blanketed all around with numerous gardens and emerald lawns. We vision them adorned with pretty Creole belles in gaily colored hooped skirt dresses.... and, as we watch, their gentlemen callers proudly promenade them around. We close our eyes and bring ourselves into those nights of the gay garland ballroom where dancing and dining can be ours in festive fashion. And the orchestra plays to us over and over our carefully selected song, until dawn wakes us from this enchanting dream.

Once again to our sentimental journey.... but wait! Before we leave we must listen to the children at play, they have so much joy together, and they note no difference because of color. Listen further to the happy voices in song that come from the fields of work. These are the happy years my darling, the years before treachery, deceit and greed twisted peaceful minds into hatreds, confusion and ugliness.

Adrift once more on this entwining snake-like stream we prepare ourselves for more enchanting adventures. Green banks of grass tell us of a showboat's visit with minstrels from afar bringing happiness into the hearts of others. Negroes and whites together have lined these banks with gaiety and song.

On down the way into a tranquil refuge we sight treasures of Acadian houses with gabled roofs that hold special distinction. Stairways reach up into the loft from wide front porches that seem to be forever covered with kinfolk.

There is so much friendliness in the air as Creole farmers and workers wave to us with joy, beckoning for us to join them for "Café Noir." Graciously we decline, "We have such a distance to our journey and we must be on our way, but we will return some day to stay awhile with you."

There are so many that greet us on the way, some on shore at work, others at play. See grandmère waving to us from the kitchen window; surely there is a custard in the oven that no one can resist. Grandpère on the porch does not see us, dozing that way with his hat covering his eyes. There are those in pirogues and in barges and those in the shrimp boats with draping nets and catches of wealth within the hold.

This land, so fertile and lush, is every farmer's dream. So many expansive gardens of corn, peas, carrots, peppers and turnips and a multitude of others produce delightful thoughts that arouse the taste buds into exploring the delicious tables of Creole and Acadian cuisines. The savory gumbos and jambalayas, boudins and country sausages, stewed chickens and crawfish bisque with rice dishes of great delight. Too numerous, too tempting are they to name so with regrets we'll just be on our way. Perhaps soon we will return to this Promised Land of joyful faces and French dishes.

In the hundreds there is God's animal life, domesticated and the wild. Grazing in the pastures beyond are horses, cows, sheep and swine. And look, there is a doe with her fawn at the edge of the woods! And her stag on cautious guard! Let us not disturb them, they are in so much peace.

Louisiana's past continues to unfold as we are again afloat, with many excitements yet to come. We pass sawmills, paper mills, sugar mills and wharfs where fish for food is sold.

Slowly once again our surroundings become so quiet and we are alone together in a world at rest. The water's surface has now broadened with a trail of sunlight near the center forming a boulevard of shaded lanes on either side. We travel the one beneath the ancient oaks.

Continued . . . .

The bayou keeps twisting back and forth in a calm and peaceful way offering many fascinating sights. There are many intriguing tales of pirate vessels that have sailed this stream with their treasures of silks and silver, having brought them here to trade for the gracious hospitality of those who were in sympathy with their plight.... and there were many.

Every curve brings new thrills so different from the last.

In panoramic opulence a new picture unfolds within our view. The waters across the way become bordered with cypress and hyacinth. A swampland to behold in all its enchantment and glorious color! From tree tops Spanish moss dips below like the graying beards of Rip Van Winkle trailing into the winds. Tangled vines wrap themselves unto each other without direction. The flowering underbrush brings brilliance to the darkened waters below. Duck-weed forms carpets of yellowish green amid thousands of palmettos. There are egrets and heron and hundreds of other birds, while the majestic eagle soars far above them all.

Here is preservation of nature in all its glory within these bounds and untouched by man, yet ours to behold. Come closer my darling, we must remain a while with these blessings from God kept here for us for hundreds of years. Look, sunning itself at water's edge is a 'gator and dozens of turtles are lined upon those logs! Look closely and you will see a mink or a muskrat and some ducks behind the cattail grass, watch them play so delightfully in freedom, they know we mean them no harm. They would let us stay here with them forever.

But, come my dear, we must leave, it is becoming late and the shadows are stretching long, the sunlight will soon be lost. We must go before the dark surrounds us, we have come to the voyage end. We have come to where the stream gently empties into treacherous currents so unbecoming to our tranquil Eden, so we will venture no further, we must return to our peace.

We have traveled this stream together for a hundred and fifty miles, where good fortunes of nature have surrounded us and our aqua gem. Let us live it again and again in our memories for years to come, and so often we shall enjoy.

Thank you dearest one, for traveling with me to this paradise of nature with so many atmospheres of beauty. Where tranquility is in evidence and where the state of wild and of the tame can live together in such harmony; where man has learned so well to reap the many rewards from a land that so freely yields of rich flavors, and where God has so generously displayed many of his beautiful treasures of art within the....

PEACEFUL SETTINGS OF .... "BAYOU TECHE."

A Tribute To The Pirogue

This, that unique way of travel
unmatched throughout our land,
Used by Caribs of South America
it found its way to Louzianne......

Serving the red men before our settlers
it was adopted by the French,
Has been in use by all Creoles
but mastered by Acadians since.

A dugout hollowed from a cypress log
by skilled and artistic hands,
Like a snake it glides above the water
and skims over dewy lands.

Measuring from twelve to fifteen feet
and three to four across,
It's flat on bottom with pointed ends
and is as stubborn as a horse.

It'll roll you, rock you and toss you around
taming the wildest men,
But once you've mastered a knack for handling
it'll serve you to your end.

Now just ask any wetland Cajun
from Ville Plate to Grand Isle,
"What's your best way of travel?"
a pirogue'll be his style.

Pay no attention to "damn Yankees"
who'll tell you it's a canoe,
Just put them to the test of proving,
tasks the pirogue can't do.

It'll take you to church on Sunday
or a courtin' in the night,
And bring you to the muskrat traps,
or clear from a 'gators fight.

It'll take you to the fais-do-do
in good old country style,
Or ride you to a Cajun wedding
on a houseboat near Belle Isle.

It'll herd the marshland cattle
in regular cow pony fashion,
And make them think they're Longhorn Texans
corralled by a rustler's passion.

It's been hitched to a horse and used as a sled
to harvest corn in season,
So just think up its any use
and a Cajun 'll give good reason.

It has proved as more than useful
for centuries over, and then,
It's always a real good bet
it'll do it again and again.

"So off with your hats to that splendid pirogue
the bayou Cajun's friend,
And drink a toast of Creole good cheer
that we'll never see its end!"

BARE-RRUMP!

GRR-RUMP!

The Wilds Of Louisiana

Opulent dense swamps, vast forests, great marshes and multitudes of lakes, bayous and rivers makes Louisiana a delightful wildlife paradise; the luxuriant "Eden of North America."

This mysterious bayou country is the land of many extremes; an over abundance of water, an over abundance of plant life, an over abundance of animals, fishes and fowl with a climate well tailored for year around requirements for them all. This is mother earth's tranquil refuge for all living things. It is a masterful piece of wildlife art fashioned by the hand of God for the good of mankind. The whole world shares in the fortunes of this great wilderness.

Each year countless tons of seafood and shellfish are taken from the fresh waters of the lakes and briny marshes. Shrimp, crabs, oysters and crawfish truly deserve that heralded recognition that is given to them; no where else on this continent is there such an enormous wealth of seafood deliciousness.

Ever since Louisiana was first settled by Europeans its people have been rewarded plentifully with lumber, furs, hides, wild fowl, fishes and animals for food, clothing and shelter. And, even long before that time many indian tribes were sharing in the treasures from Louisiana's nature.

Early frontiersmen lived from the wild alone, and even today, as it was then, there are trappers who move their entire families into the marshlands and swamps, all sharing and contributing to a livelihood from the pelts of their traps. Harvested furs are shipped to great cities throughout the world; muskrat, mink, otter and raccoon topping the list. Hard work was then and still is a way of life for the trapper. Many a generation has known no other way since their forefathers arrived in this bewitching wilderness.

The seemingly monotonous terrain of the gigantic marshlands can be misleading to the unknowing observer; peace and solitudes within the bayous, swamps and lakes often does not reflect realities of those enormous nurseries and havens where thousands upon thousands of wild creatures skillfully camouflage themselves from the invading predator.

There are bass, sac-a-lait, trout and perch; calico, mullet and carp. There's warmouth, croakers, bream and drum; red snapper, bluegill, catfish and flounder. There are sailfish, lemonfish, tarpon and shark. These are only a few, there are many many more to satisy great appetites and sporting minds.

Bird-life is forever so plentiful. Nearly one-third of all of North American birds are either permanent or at least winter residents of the great Louisiana refuge. There are many species of ducks, geese, hawks and egrets. Familiar winged life are quail, woodcock, doves, snipe, rails, coot, crows, heron and many more. And, then there is the familiar turkey. At any one given time there are over four hundred species of birds within Louisiana borders, with hundreds of thousands of each species.

Repitles are in various forms and countless numbers; snakes, poisonous and otherwise, frogs, turtles, lizards and, of course, the ever-reigning king of swamplands, the American alligator.

There are multitudes of fur bearers throughout the wilderness, beaver, raccoon and mink; otter, muskrat and opossum; skunk, rabbit and squirrel. The bear, the deer, the bobcat and fox all acting out their part in that great outdoor theatre of Louisiana's fascinating wild. All contributing to the well-being of each other and to the health, happiness and prosperity of man.

Yes, God has blessed Louisiana and its people with this scenic wonderland of fertile soils, prairies, woods, marshes, swamps, lakes, rivers, bayous and numerous varieties of animals and plants to fill them with. And, God has blessed her with a grateful humankind who can truly appreciate the many gifts bestowed upon them in this vast, mysterious "Land O' Plenty."

> *"Lush perfumed woodlands embellished with lakes, rivers, bayous and an abundance of fruit, nuts and wildlife became a fabulous paradise refuge for pioneering strangers from distant lands."*

NATURE'S WONDERLAND

Nature's Wonderland

The early morning ground fog
        burns into atmosphere,
Yellow golds and greens are lighted
        as day begins to clear.

Cool breezes wake the Spanish moss
        into swaying pendulums from trees,
Life beings to unfold from night
        of undisturbed refreshing ease.

The 'gator's croak is warning all
        that he is ready for a meal,
While white-tailed buck keeps away
        in fear of that appeal.

The egret's alarmed by fluttering wings
        of an arriving mallard friend,
And Mrs. Heron listens o'er sounds
        for calls her mate may send.

Old ruffled eagle scowls at noises
        so very early in the day,
"How can anything wake this hour?"
        he can be heard to say.

The slow to rise cottonmouth
        is a meal for otter today,
And grizzle coated "coony" begins
        his cappers of clownish play.

Wilderness is a bustle of energy
        with all alive on the bayou bed,
Garfish and cats state the fact
        the wild is waiting to be fed.

So scamper little crawfish, be aware
        of intruding predators skills,
Nudge Mr. Turtle to be alert
        this will be a day of thrills.

Continued . . . .

That tempermental snobbish mink
    with his highly valued fur,
May be around the next tree stump,
    with the greatest appetite ashore.

So caution is the general word
    that goes out into the swamp,
Survival is a way of life
    for those of careless romp.

These are the scenes of the wild
    and happening everyday,
In Louisiana's wonderlands where
    NATURE HAS HER WAY.

Spanish Moss

It is neither Spanish nor is it a moss. Strangely, it is an air plant of the pineapple family that uses tree branches only as mechanical supports for its existence. It does not destroy plant life, it is not a parasite that receives its nutrients from other plants. These swaying festoons are very charming embellishments to the forests, swamps and countrysides.

Early French settlers in Louisiana were fascinated with this beard-like growth hanging from the trees and called it "Spanish Beards." They later changed the name to Spanish moss. Native indians referred to it as "tree hair" and from this botanists gave it the Greek name "Dendropogran," meaning simply, "tree hair."

For a long time Spanish moss was a source of income for many swamp dwellers who collected it for moss gins. At the gin it was washed, combed of twigs and debris, dried and packed into bales to be shipped to manufacturing plants all over the world. It was used as mattress stuffing, upholstering for chairs, padding for horse collars and carriage seats. Among other uses, colonial builders used Spanish moss to bind together the clay packs between the walls of their homes. This "bousillage" construction furnished incredible insulating qualities.

When properly cured the inner black fibers of the moss are exposed and takes on spring-like resilience that becomes very tough and durable. There is hardly a chemical matter that can destroy the properties of the cured product.

Spanish moss grows just about anywhere in southern Louisiana, along roads, byways and deep into forests and swamps. It casts glamorous canopies over great ancient trees giving an eerie charm to the scenery, leaving indelible impressions upon the minds of visitors.

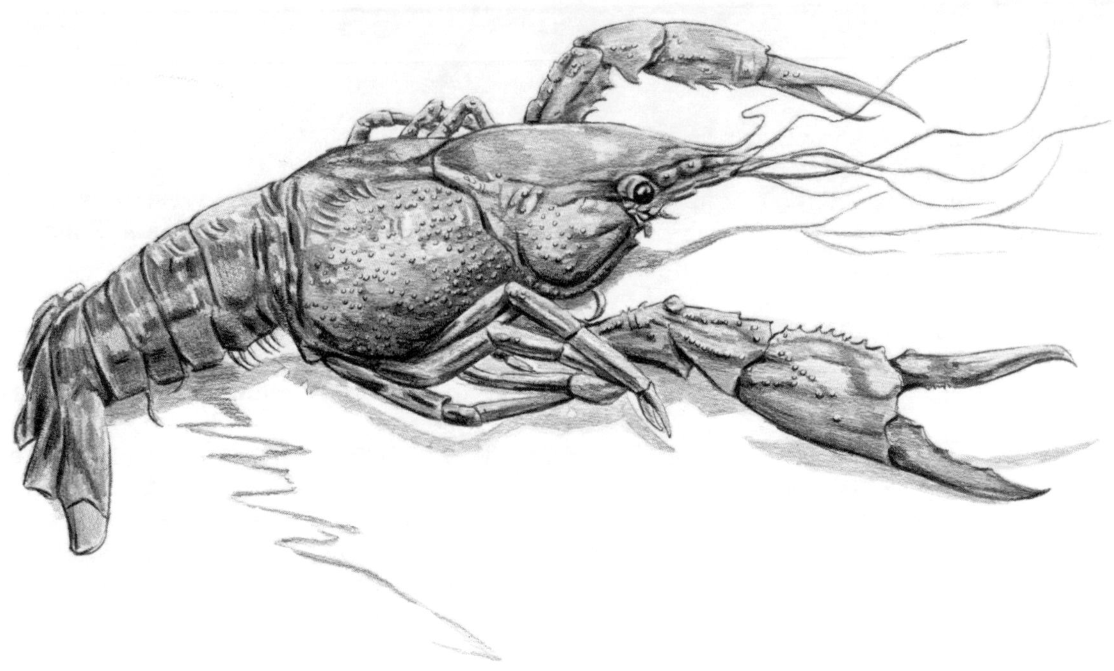

Mr. Crawfish

In the lowlands of Louisiana where waters are shallow and dense, this little gentleman slowly crawls his way around the bottoms eagerly awaiting those who come to embrace him as a delicacy for the table. He is a loveable little guy with pincers, whiskers and fantail who adorns the plates of everyone privileged to know him. He is a miniature of a lobster with flavors of richness second to none in shellfish. With proud modesty he turns a blushing red in the iron pots of seasoned waters giving him a charm, character and taste like no other. And his greatest delights are the smiling and joyous faces of all ages who look upon him with pleasure. With active taste buds and generous appetites all are willing to grant him his wish of being worthy of his existence. MR. CRAWFISH, the delightful little character of the lush Louisiana swamplands!

"Crabby"

This aggressive little creature bullies his way along the water beds with an unbalanced rudder that makes him move forward "sideways." He grows to a wide edible range of sizes often measured from twelve to as many as forty-eight to the dozen. Arm yourself with string, net, pole, lots of bait and strong determination 'cause you're gonna try hard to get him. He's no fool, a crafty lil' critter that will cut your string, steal your bait, fight back at ya and pincer your nets. But, he's worth all the efforts; his firmly packed white meat enhanced in taste with lemon juice, hot sauces, beer and French bread is as delicious a meal as can be devoured.

J DeHart

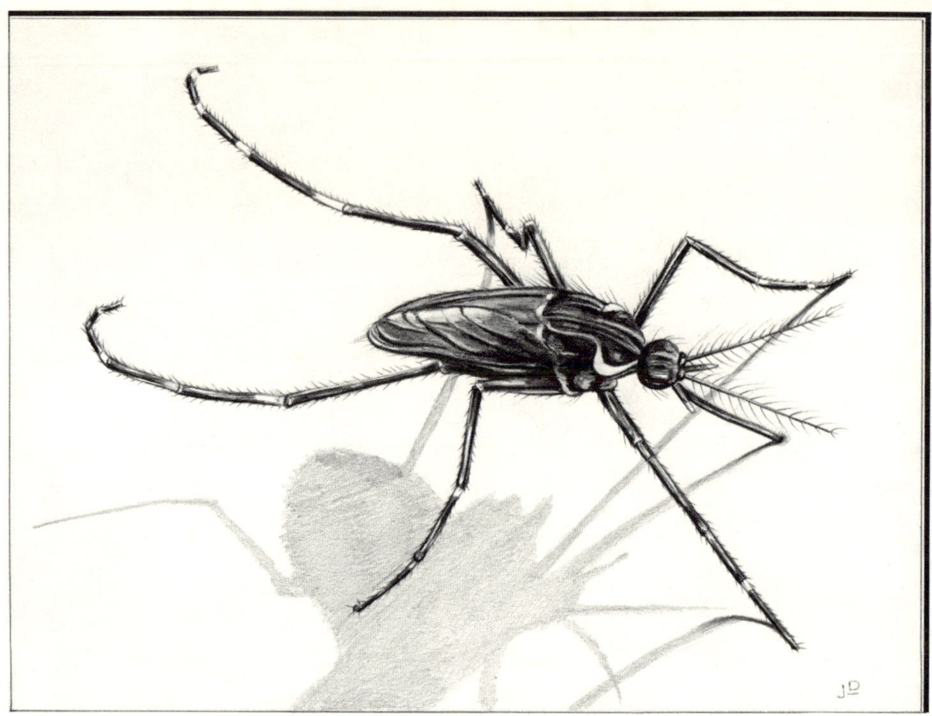

Maringouin

Louisiana pioneers and Creole ancestors who developed Louisiana into one of America's finest and most productive states did so not without many setbacks, discomforts and sadness.

There were violent hardships when encountering hostile indians and there were countless dangers from the swamp and beasts of prey in nearby jungles.

There has been failures of crops time over again due to droughts, too much rain or by the winged and animal predator devouring all within a day and night. And, there were treacherous hurricanes, winds and floodwaters that wiped out previous accomplishments. But, the Creoles have survived these with even more determination and rebound.

Other than the Civil War, perhaps the most devastating of setbacks and life-taking enemies to civilization in Louisiana were the horrifying epidemics of yellow fever. It appeared in widespread fashion thirty-nine times between the years of 1796 and 1906. An epidemic often lasted months, taking untold counts in human lives.

In New Orleans alone people died by the thousands, once it was upon them there was no way to combat the fever. Seemingly healthy families dined happily together at night and on the following morning all were found together in death from the fever. Hundreds of such cases have occurred.

Piles of bodies lined the streets and mounted so quickly it was impossible to bury them in proper fashion, so they were either burned in masses or laid to rest in trench graves without coffin or headstones.

Discovering the cause of such devastating fevers, open ditches were coated with oil and salt until proper coverings could be installed, rainwater cisterns were covered with screens, and with caution directed to incoming ships in port the terrible *Maringuoin* could no longer breed, bringing to end that carrier of horrors, sufferings and death.

THE END OF AN ERA

J DeHart

Embers From Civil War Flames

History books seldom do reveal,
true versions do not unfold,
Those wrathful intents and loathsome
aftermaths were never ever told.
So, cup your hands behind your ears, just
listen..... listen to the sounds of the past,
Shade your eyes from untrue visions
and look to truth at last.

* * *

Opulence once reigned throughout the Southland
posing serious political threats,
While masses were still in Yankee favor,
WAR!.... perhaps could stem regrets.
Governing powers were greatly envious
"The flourishing South they must destroy!"
Dissension must be created, using *SLAVERY* as the tool
and *HATE* could be a toy!

Killing, raping and violent ravagement of farmland and
abode.... destroying all shelter, food and stock,
Whites and blacks without home, left in total famine,
a pathetic and hopeless flock.
Overnight, monuments of heritage and lifetimes of human
toil vanished into shambles and strife,
Irreparable losses were suffered and heavy garments of
grief wrapped multitudes for life.

Both, blacks and whites wore faces of sadness,
many promises never did come,
Misfortunes weighed heavily about, losses were grave....
overpowering numbers had won.
The victor became quite indifferent to negroes
who had come to ask for help,
With envies appeased by conquest, blacks were turned southward
.....compassion was never felt.

Continued ....

When tool and toy had served a purpose
	promising fathers turned them away,
Returning home, negroes gained no refuge from loathsome
	carpetbaggers, 'twas a sad and resentful day.
Throngs of blacks found themselves unwanted and adrift....
	they had no place to descend,
Southern planters took them in, and as before,
	together they sought to mend.

The victor gave nothing but loudly heralded
	promises.... nothing but blood, tears and hates,
But, southern whites and blacks gathered the remnants
	and toiled to fashion new fates.
Recovery was very slow, but pioneering spirits of
	ancestors firmed their resolutions,
Faith in God grew even stronger, easing their burdens,
	guiding them to solutions.

Embers continued to burn long after the flames had died,
	leaving only the ashes of their labors,
Yet, sorrows and hardships that lingered for generations
	brought unity to friends and neighbors.
That Golden Era had come to an end, and,
	for many decades a giant lay quietly asleep,
But now, growing signs of refreshed awakenings
	show fruitful harvests to be reaped.

New horizons have appeared in southern skies,
	with numerous goals to obtain,
And, with happy hearts and beaming faces
	THE SOUTH WILL RISE AGAIN!

GLOSSARY

AFFAIRES D'AMOUR - Affairs of love.

AMANTS DE MARDI GRAS - Mardi Gras Lovers.

LES AMERICAINS - Louisianians of English descent who migrated from the north-eastern and mid-western United States after the Louisiana Purchase.

BAMBOULA - A dance executed to the accompaniment of a primitive African drum.

BANQUETTE - A sidewalk or walkway.

BELVEDERE - A railed platform on a rooftop, often with a cupola.

"BIG HOUSE" - Main residence of a plantation.

BOUILLABAISSE - A highly seasoned stew made with several kinds of fish and seafood.

BOUSILLAGE - Inner walls packed with a mixture of mud and deer hair or moss. An excellent insulation.

CAFÉ AU LAIT - Coffee prepared with hot milk.

CAFÉ BRÛLOT - Hot coffee prepared with spices, citrus and flaming brandy.

CAFÉ DU CHICKORY - A blend of coffee and ground roasted chickory root.

CAFÉ DU MONDE - Coffee with friends.

CAFÉ NOIR - Strong black coffee prepared by slow drip method.

CAJUN - A popular corruption for the word Acadian.

CALINDA - A dance of African origin done by slaves of Louisiana.

CAMELBACK - A house with single story in front and two stories at the rear.

CONGRIS (Voodoo term) - Black-eyed peas and rice cooked with sugar.

COURTBOUILLON - Redfish stew cooked in highly seasoned gravy.

CREOLE - A white descendant of pure European French and Spanish settlers of Louisiana.

CUISINIERE - French household cook.

CUITE - A thick syrup from the sugarhouse taken just before it turns to sugar. Also known as "sugarhouse candy."

CREVASSE - A break in a levee causing flooding conditions.

FAIS-DODO (Pronounced "fay dough-dough) - A country dance popular with the Cajuns of southern Louisiana.

FE CHAUFFEE - A voodoo ritual dance where the women remove all their clothing except chemises and dance with candles attached to the top of their heads.

FILLES Á LA CASSETTE - Casket Girls (see Ursulines of New Orleans).

FLAMBEAU - A torch used by escorts to light the way for a carnival parade.

FLAMME D'JOYEAUX - Fire of joy. Burning pyramids of logs atop the levee on Christmas Eve.

FLAMME DE LA LEGENDE JOYEUSE - Flame of Joy Legend.

GALLERY - A large porch.

GARÇONNIÈRE - Bachelors quarters, usually seperate from the main house.

GRAND JOUR DE FÊTE - A grand festival day.

GRENIER - An attic.

GRIS-GRIS - A voodoo charm to ward off or inflict evil.

GUMBO - A thick soup prepared with a roux, okra, seafood, sausages, ham, veal or chicken.

GUMBO FRENCH - A patois of French with Negro slangs.

JAMBALAYA - Rice cooked with either shrimp, sausage, chicken or other ingredients. A mixture of many things.

KREWES - Private social clubs that organize, develop and produce Mardi Gras balls, parades and other carnival season events.

LA FÊTE DU COCHON - The festival of the pig.
LAGNIAPPE (Pronounced "lan-yap") - A little extra given to customer by merchants to show appreciation for business received.

MARDI GRAS - "Fat Tuesday," the last day of Carnival season. The day before the religious holiday Ash Wednesday.
LA MESSE DE MINUIT - Midnight Mass on Christmas Eve.
MULATTO - An offspring of a Negro and a caucasian.
MARINGOUIN - A mosquito.

PAPA LA BAS (Voodoo term) - King of devils, ruling voodoo spirit in the guise of a serpent.
PARISH - A governmental district of Louisiana known elsewhere as a county.
PIGEONNIER - A pigeon house for raising squab on a French plantation.
PORTE COCHÈRE - A carriageway entrance to a courtyard.
POUSSEE CAFÉ - A drink of different liqueurs in layers.
PRALINE - A candy made with pecans and boiled sugar.

QUADROON - An offspring of a mulatto and a caucasian. A person of one-fourth Negro blood.

RE COLTE SAISON - Harvest Season.
ROUX - A sauce of flour browned in butter or lard and seasoned. A roux is an important base for numerous Creole dishes.

SAISON ACCUEILS - Season Greetings.
SHOTGUN HOUSE - A long narrow house in which the rooms are one behind the other, unique to Louisiana.
SOIRÉE - An evening party.
SPASM BAND - An orchestra with make-shift soapbox instruments accompanied by tap dancers. Usually young Negroes who perform in the streets of the French Quarter in New Orleans.

TAFIA - A drink made with rum and sugar cane juices.
TIGNON - A headpiece made with a bright-colored handkerchief.

VIEUX CARRÉ - Old Square. Originally the walled-in section of old New Orleans, now known as the French Quarter.
VOODOO - An African cult practiced by Louisiana Negro slaves. Sorcery.
VOODOO GUMBO - A stew made from various live animals, supposedly to enhance sexual desires during voodoo rituals.

WANGO - A material object or a spirit used to cast a voodoo spell. Similar to a gris-gris.

ZOMBI - A voodoo spirit, a voodoo snake.

THE AUTHOR

Writer/Illustrator Jess DeHart is a native of Louisiana with a Creole heritage that is deeply rooted into Louisiana's rich history. The literary and art work of this book represents just a small portion of the many hundreds of writings, drawings and paintings that he has made during his long career as an artist. His paintings include a wide variety of subjects; historic, human, animal, landscape, seascape and wildlife.

Most of the drawings shown in HALLMARKS OF A HERITAGE are pencil studies for paintings that Jess DeHart has already made or for others that he is planning for the future. His works are in numerous private collections throughout the United States.

Besides the many months of studio work required for the writing and illustrating of a book, Mr. DeHart and his wife travel thousands of miles and spends countless hours of library research, on-the-scene interviews, making notes, sketches and taking photographs.... gathering information that can later be used in his studio work.

Other books of historic nature written and illustrated by Jess DeHart include "Plantations of Louisiana" and "Louisiana's Historic Towns."